Forest *Hill*
LOUISIANA

Forest Hill
LOUISIANA

A BLOOM TOWN HISTORY

CHERÉ DASTUGUE COEN

Foreword by MAYOR CHARLES "CHUCK" ELLIOTT

THE
History
PRESS

Published by The History Press
Charleston, SC 29403
www.historypress.net

First published 2014

Manufactured in the United States

ISBN 978.1.62619.701.5

Library of Congress CIP data applied for.

Contents

Foreword, by Charles "Chuck" Elliott   7
Acknowledgements   9
Introduction   11

1. The Early Settlement of Forest Hill   17
2. The Timber Industry   35
3. Forest Hill Becomes a Town   53
4. The Great Outdoors   65
5. The Depression Years   71
6. Camp Claiborne and World War II   81
7. Growth of the Nursery Industry   93
8. The Boom Years   111
9. Taking Over Education   121
10. Forest Hill Today   127
11. Notable Forest Hill Residents   139

Appendix: Forest Hill Churches and Cemeteries   147
Notes   153
Bibliography   159
Index   169
About the Author   175

Foreword

The nursery industry in central Louisiana began very slowly in the mid- to late 1890s. At that time, the lumber and sawmill industries—along with "traditional" farming—were the predominant sources of livelihood for the area's residents. It wasn't until the 1940s and 1950s that the development and growth of a new type of farming blossomed. By then, World War II and the decline of the local sawmills had disrupted the historical lifestyle and provided the opportunity (and need) for alternative means to support family life.

Since then, through persistence and innovation, local nursery owners have revolutionized the industry. Today, some estimates suggest that the nursery industry now generates more than $150 million in annual revenues from the more than two hundred nurseries in central Louisiana. Those estimates do not consider the ancillary businesses that have developed in support of the nursery owners, including agricultural chemicals and supplies businesses; greenhouse forms and supplies; liner, mulch, soil, plant container, rock gravel and other suppliers; welders; mechanics; gas and oil distributors; landscapers; and financial institutions.

This book documents the history of central Louisiana's nursery industry and its important contributions to Forest Hill and areas near and far. In a magnificent job of research and presentation, Cheré Coen honors those individuals, both past and present, who have contributed so much of their lives to the industry's success. We hope that you will enjoy this historical perspective. May God bless you, one and all.

CHARLES "CHUCK" ELLIOTT
Mayor, Forest Hill, Louisiana

Acknowledgements

L ittle has been written formally about Forest Hill, Louisiana, so I'm deeply indebted to those who helped me piece together the history of this small but enterprising village. Thanks first to Mayor Charles Elliott for his endless support and resources and to his wonderful staff at city hall, particularly Grace McMillan and Cheryl Cloessner.

The nursery owners who spent time to patiently explain the business and history, not to mention the horticultural information such as liners and grafting techniques, were invaluable; thanks to Mike and Inez Polakovich and Chris and Cathy Jo Polakovich; Estelle and Harold Poole; Sam and Donna Stokes and Rodney and Doris Stokes; J.J. and Ann Jeter; Marcia Young; Stanley Young; Clyde Holloway; George, Vera and Murphy Johnson; and to the nurseries who e-mailed and mailed me information about their businesses. Thanks also to Irma Rodriguez and Eddie Ponce for their input on the Hispanic community of Forest Hill; to Richard Crowell for his information about the lumber industry; to Roger Butter for his heartfelt memoirs; and to Sheldon Blue, Donna Christianson and Betsy Palmer for their personal experiences.

Thanks also to Dale Genius, director and curator of the Louisiana History Museum; Richard Moran, curator of the Louisiana Maneuvers and Military Museum; the Louisiana State Library; and the Alexandria Public Library—all archives of valuable information. And a special thanks to Everett Lueck of the Southern Forest Heritage Museum, who spent a day explaining not only the timber industry and its influence on the area but also where every railroad roadbed, gravel pit and lumber dry kiln was located within a fifty-mile radius of Forest Hill.

I'm also eternally grateful for Solomon Northup, who wrote at great length about the Forest Hill area in his haunting memoir *Twelve Years a Slave*, and for Louisiana State University–Alexandria professor Sue Lyles Eakin for bringing Northup's story and the places he lived to life, in addition to her other many history books on Rapides Parish. First-person narratives make history come alive.

And finally, thanks to my family for putting up with me during the writing of this book. There are few people more disagreeable than a writer on deadline.

Introduction

Driving north on Interstate 49 through the heart of Louisiana, the terrain changes shortly past Bunkie. Prairies dotted with sprawling live oak trees and rice fields filled with crawfish buckets quickly turn to rolling hills and dense pine forests. Turn right at Exit 66 and the hills disappear, replaced by the flat alluvial plains of the Red River, where once plantations grew cotton and sugar cane as far as the eye could see. Head west from I-49 and the hills continue, the highway rolling through acres of what gardeners consider a Louisiana heaven.

At first glance, the town of Forest Hill appears as little more than a moment at a traffic light. Before visitors connect with U.S. Highway 165, another main thoroughfare to Lake Charles or Alexandria, they'll spot the Forest Hill City Hall, the volunteer fire department, a small collection of businesses—including one bank and a barbershop—and a delightful municipal park with a pond at its center. A few streets over is the elementary school and the former high school's gymnasium, now being used as a senior citizens center. Scattered here and there are the handful of churches and cemeteries tucked within the woods.

And then there are the more than two hundred plant nurseries. Without the acres and acres of plant nurseries greeting visitors on the way into town, Forest Hill would just be another small, rural Louisiana town. Instead, it's home to a multimillion-dollar industry. Even more surprising, the population of Forest Hill hovers near nine hundred residents, while the number of plant nurseries in the town and surrounding areas has

Forest Hill is nestled among the piney woods of central Louisiana. *Cheré Coen.*

been well over two hundred for at least a few decades. The recent recession took a small bite out of the trade, which saw its heyday in the '80s and '90s and depends largely on the housing industry, but business is still blooming in Forest Hill, a pun that's routinely popular in newspaper and magazine headlines.

The history of Forest Hill predates the nursery industry, with economics in the piney woods demanding constant reinvention. Small farmers and timber mill owners moved into the region in the nineteenth century, but the soil wasn't as conducive to farming as the rich loam to the east near the town of Lecompte, where plantations were built on Red River floodplains and slave labor cotton drew a high price at market. Fortunes were made along Bayou Boeuf south of Alexandria, so settlement in the piney woods in and around present-day Forest Hill was slow to come by, except by hardy souls who started farms and plantation owners who visited the pine forests to escape the destructive fevers of summer.

After the Civil War, the economy shifted for those growing cotton on Bayou Boeuf plantations, although prosperity for Forest Hill was still decades away. Where thoughts of taking advantage of the great virgin pine forests to the west had crossed minds in the early and mid-nineteenth century, ideas on milling these acres of opportunity only took shape with the advent of railroads and investors in the latter part of the century. Once the Kansas City, Watkins and Gulf Railway pushed through the area in 1892, establishing a depot at Forest Hill, a new era began. The prosperous timber industry roared through the piney woods as fast as a forest fire with this new avenue of shipping lumber to market, and in many ways it was just as destructive upon its conclusion. For years, jobs were plenty, and towns sprung up almost overnight to satisfy the sawmills and their ever-roaring blades slicing massive longleaf pine into lumber.

In 1897, Forest Hill officially became a town, with citizens working at a number of sawmills in the area, including the large Long Leaf complex and two major mills at McNary. Gravel pits began operating as well, and railroad spurs traversed the woods in all directions. "It was an industrial complex," said Everett Lueck, president of the board at the Southern Forest Heritage Museum, located just outside Forest Hill.

By the 1920s, however, the timber was spent, acres in all directions clear-cut and devoid of the majestic longleaf pine trees. With the elimination of forests came the abandonment of the lumber companies, many packing up shop and leaving the region, if not Louisiana. Forest Hill residents were forced to regroup, return to farming or head to the gravel pits.

One entrepreneur, Samuel Stokes, had a better idea. A lover of plants and nature, Stokes found interesting species in the piney woods near his home, plants such as rare dogwoods, camellias and azaleas. He taught himself horticulture and learned to graft, propagating the central Louisiana native plants first for his own enjoyment and then to sell to others. He discovered pansies and ways to grow hundreds of the colorful flowers on his property for an eager market throughout the country. Within years, Stokes had a booming nursery business.

Forest Hill residents also found new opportunities with the Civilian Conservation Corps, which arrived to alleviate the devastation to the soil brought on by unregulated timber practices. A state fish hatchery was built, and tourists visited the area's watering holes, such as Shady Nook, and fishing meccas Indian Creek Dam and Cocodrie Lake. In the meantime, Stokes taught others his nursery business, residents such as Baker Taylor, Billy Mitchell and the Poole brothers (Murphy Archie Poole and Hayden Johns Poole Sr.); the industry slowly began to grow.

By 1940, the economy of Forest Hill—and Rapides Parish—had shifted again. Troops training for combat in World War II came roaring through the region much like the timber industry had done, with 500,000 troops visiting the temporary military base of Camp Claiborne just a few short miles north of Forest Hill from 1940 to 1946. The town enjoyed prosperity instantly, feeding off the military base and its temporary inhabitants until, like the loss of virgin forest, the soldiers were gone.

Once again, Forest Hill was forced to reinvent itself, and it found its stride in a new and exciting venture. Residents began working for the Stokes and the Poole Brothers Nurseries, learning the trade and opening their own nurseries in turn. New generations came along to take their parents' places, branching out like a genealogy tree and marrying into other nursery families.

The Central Louisiana Association of Nurserymen was organized to promote networking and cost-saving measures among the nursery owners, and the growing industry started attracting nursery distributors and other associated businesses.

By the 1980s, Forest Hill owned a thriving plant nursery industry, one that inspired the Louisiana legislature to label it the "Nursery Capital of Louisiana." Plants grown in Forest Hill traveled throughout Louisiana and its surrounding states, with some sold as far as the East Coast, and many ended up on shelves of big-box stores such as Lowe's, Home Depot and Walmart. Every spring, thousands would flock to the piney woods town for the popular Louisiana Nursery Festival.

The great American success story continued with the Hispanic community of Forest Hill, workers who arrived from Mexico as seasonal workers to fill a labor shortage, learned the trade and opened their own nurseries, much as the early Forest Hill residents had done.

Today, the success story that is Forest Hill lines Highways 112 and 165, pouring into neighboring towns such as Glenmora, Woodworth, McNary and Lecompte. Even nurseries located in adjacent parishes have ties to the horticultural town, connected to one another through a unique sharing of business. Some nurseries such as Stokes date back one hundred years or more, while others are newcomers to the trade.

The small town of Forest Hill, Louisiana, contains and is surrounded by more than two hundred plant nurseries. *Cheré Coen.*

At first glance, Forest Hill appears as another miniature, rural Louisiana town nestled in the state's piney wood forests. Children attend the local elementary, parents deposit their money at the Red River bank branch and residents pay their municipal bills at the small windowed office at city hall. On Sundays, voices raise up in a handful of churches.

Just behind the small-town façade, however, lies a massive green industry, its rows of woody ornamentals, trees and flowers branching off from the center of town for thousands of acres into the horizon.

As the headlines sporting puns note, Forest Hill is a bloom town.

CHAPTER 1

The Early Settlement of Forest Hill

It's difficult to name the original inhabitants of the Forest Hill area. Most of the American Indians who resided in Rapides Parish fall into several original tribes before European settlement and a diverse set when Europeans drove the first inhabitants westward. The tribal makeup changed constantly.

"With the coming of the Europeans, Indians in the area around the [Red River] rapids were pushed westward and replaced by other Indians pushed from points further east," wrote Sue Eakin in *Rapides Parish History*. "Finally, only clusters of Indians in small villages stayed around the curves of the Bayou Boeuf and along Indian Creek or in the vicinity of Glenmore until they too moved out of the area sometime during the early years of the nineteenth century."

Eakin names Pascagoulas, Caddoans in the northern hill country of the parish and the Avoyel tribe to the south around Marksville in Avoyelles Parish as original native groups living in Rapides Parish. Some historians claim that a band of Choctaws lived in the Appalaches Village in what is now Zimmerman, as well as in a line south/southeast to Pine Prairie. Louisiana historian G.P. Whittington cites an early French official's claim that the Chickasaws took advantage of travelers when the Red River rapids were at their worst, that a tribe of Attakapas lived to the south and east of Lake Cocodrie and that Choctaws arrived in central Louisiana sometime in the eighteenth century, with a small tribe established on Bayou Beouf.[1] The Yowani Choctaws were believed to have lived in central Louisiana as early

Cocodrie Lake, south of Forest Hill. *State Library of Louisiana.*

as the mid-1750s, eventually moving from a village on Bayou Chicot into the Clifton community. Other sites of Choctaw settlements were believed to have existed at Boyce, Flatwoods, Clifton Crossing, Hineston, Seiper Creek and Woodworth.[2]

"The Biloxi Chatot, and other Pascagoula and Yowani began moving to lands along Bayou Rapides and Bayou Boeuf" in the late nineteenth century, according to the authors of *The Historic Indian Tribes of Louisiana.* "The Alabama and some Choctaw had established settlements near Chicot and Cocodrie, in present-day central Louisiana, and the Pacana settled near present-day Elizabeth, on the headwaters of the Calcasieu River." The authors also claim that the Choctaws displaced some native tribes in the region, such as the Adai west of Natchitoches, and took up residence "south of Bayou Boeuf near Indian Creek at Woodworth and Glenmore."

"The Choctaw lived in the lowlands and later moved to Indian Creek (near Lecompte), Hicks and Zimmerman," wrote Don C. Marler in *Historic Hineston.* "These Indians were thought to be Yowani Choctaws."

During the 1930s, the Works Progress Administration of President Franklin D. Roosevelt included a series of reports called the Louisiana Writers Project. Louisiana writers traveled throughout the state, documenting histories of communities and people and compiling collections of folklore, legends and oral histories. One account focused on Ashton Plantation, located west of Lamourie and northwest of Lecompte, only a few miles from Forest Hill. "Ashton plantation is a part of the Miller and Fulton land acquired from the Pascagoula, Appalachi and Alabami Indians in 1802. Some of these Indians were known to have lived around Lemourie [*sic*] prior to 1783. Relics of an Indian village have been found on this property in recent years."[3]

Another account claimed that a tribe of friendly Choctaws lived in the vicinity of present-day Forest Hill along Spring Creek and Hurricane Creek and down toward Lake Cocodrie. "These Choctaw Indians cultivated small fields of corn and made split cane baskets, dyed in bright colors, which were sold in Alexandria. They also sold game and deer skins. The deer skins which they dressed were of a superior quality and it was generally believed that the Indians used a secret formula for curing the buck skins."[4]

Perhaps the best-known record and a first-person account of American Indians living in the Forest Hill area comes from Solomon Northup, a free man of color who wrote a memoir of being kidnapped and sold into slavery to a central Louisiana plantation owner. In his book *Twelve Years a Slave: Narrative of Solomon Northup, a Citizen of New York, Kidnapped in Washington City in 1841, and Rescued in 1853*, Northup described the tribal members he met in the woods near Indian Creek, where his owner, William Prince Ford, operated a sawmill:

> *Indian Creek, in its whole length, flows through a magnificent forest. There dwells on its shore a tribe of Indians, a remnant of the Chickasaws or Chickopees, if I remember rightly. They live in simple huts, ten or twelve feet square, constructed of pine poles and covered with bark. They subsist primarily on the flesh of the deer, the coon, and opossum, all of which are plenty in these woods. Sometimes they exchange venison for a little corn and whiskey with the planters on the bayou. Their usual dress is buckskin breeches and calico hunting shirts of fantastic colors, buttoned from belt to chin. They wear brass rings on their wrists, and in their ears and noses. The dress of the squaws is very similar. They are fond of dogs and horses— owning many of the latter, of a small, tough breed—and are skillful riders. Their bridles, girths and saddles were made of raw skins of animals; their stirrups of a certain kind of wood. Mounted astride their ponies, men and women, I have seen them dash out into the woods at the utmost of their speed, following narrow winding paths, and dodging trees, in a manner that eclipsed the most miraculous feats of civilized equestrianism. Circling away in various directions, the forest echoing and reechoing with their whoops, they would presently return at the same dashing, headlong speed with which they started. Their village was on Indian Creek, known as Indian Castle, but their range extended to the Sabine River. Occasionally a tribe from Texas would come over on a visit, and then there was indeed*

a carnival in the "Great Pine Woods." Chief of the tribe was Cascalla; second in rank, John Baltese, his son-in-law; with both of whom, as with many others of the tribe, I became acquainted during my frequent voyages down the creek with rafts…. They were obedient with the chief; the word of Cascalla was their law. They were a rude but harmless people, and enjoyed their wild mode of life. They had little fancy for the open country, the cleared lands on the shores of the bayous, but preferred to hide themselves within the shadows of the forest. They worshipped the Great Spirit, loved whisky, and were happy.

Northup witnessed a dance "when a roving herd from Texas had encamped in their village." The entire deer was roasting on a large fire, and the tribal members formed a ring, with the "men and squaws alternately," and played a tune on what Northup describe as "a sort of Indian fiddle":

At the first note, if indeed there was more than one note in the whole tune, they circled around, trotting after each other, and giving utterance to a guttural, sing-song noise, equally as nondescript as the music of the fiddle. At the end of the third circuit, they would stop suddenly, whoop as if their lungs would crack, then break from the ring, forming in couples, man and squaw, each jumping backwards as far as possible from the other, then forwards—which graceful feat having been twice or thrice accomplished, they would form in a ring, and go trotting round again. The best dancer appeared to be considered the one who could whoop the loudest, jump the farthest, and utter the most excruciating noise. At intervals, one or more would leave the dancing circle, and going to the fire, cut from the roasting carcass a slice of venison.

In a hole, shaped like a mortar, cut in the trunk of a fallen tree, they pounded corn with a wooden pestle, and of the meal made cake. Alternately they danced and ate. Thus were the visitors from Texas entertained by the dusky sons and daughters of the Chicopees, and such is a description, as I saw it, of an Indian ball in the Pine Woods of Avoyelles.[5]

A recurring legend about Forest Hill and its Native American ancestry is that the town existed on an old Choctaw village. "Forest Hill is on the site of an early Choctaw village," according to *Louisiana: A Guide to the State*, compiled by the Writers' Program of the Works Progress Administration. "The Indians were friendly with the white settlers, whom they supplied with woven split-cane baskets dyed in bright colors, and leather cured and worked to extraordinary softness. About the middle of the nineteenth century the Indians abandoned the site, and the whites began to form a village, later named Bismark. When the railroad was built through in 1890, Forest Hill was substituted for Bismark."

Another legend claims that the Choctaw village existed close to present-day Lake Cocodrie. The Choctaw men of the village left to hunt, leaving the women and children by the side of the creek. While the men were gone, the land beneath the creek collapsed, and the waters rose quickly, forming a lake and drowning the tribe's women and children. The men were so devastated that they left the area, refusing to visit that section of Rapides Parish again.

"The Indians abandoned it about the middle of the nineteenth century," related Clare D'Artois Leeper in *Louisiana Place Names*.

EUROPEANS ARRIVE

Early French settlers of Louisiana gravitated to Natchitoches, an outpost established in 1714 in order to trade with neighboring American Indians and the Spanish who resided to the west. New Orleans followed as a poste in 1718, a viable port city on the Mississippi River with quick access to Lake Pontchartrain and the Gulf of Mexico.

Just south of the Natchitoches Poste, Rapides Parish remained undeveloped for decades, mostly a territory where settlers traveled to and from Natchitoches, New Orleans and the later developed Opelousas Poste. Early on, however, Frenchman Diron d'Artequette suggested that a fort be built at "le grand rapide," referring to the limestone ledge stretching over the Red River that created rapids during high waters. This proposed fortress would help protect Fort St. Jean Baptiste at Natchitoches, he insisted. No true development began until the Spanish took over Louisiana in 1762, when France ceded the Isle of Orleans and all of Louisiana west of the Mississippi to Spain in the Treaty of Fontainebleau.

"The opinion of this writer is that the establishment of a post was made at the rapids of the Red River not until the beginning of the Spanish regime; thus, local records prior to such a time never would have existed," wrote historian Winston DeVille in his *Rapides Post on Red River: Census and Military Documents for Central Louisiana, 1769–1800*. "Indeed, we know of no records in French archives which indicate in any way that there was any kind of establishment at Rapides during the French period—not even a few military men or a priest. The question is worth exploring, for the day when the site at the rapids became Rapides Post has never been satisfactorily resolved."

With Louisiana now under Spanish rule, the Spanish renamed the post *El Rapido*, again for the rapids above present-day Alexandria and Pineville that were "an impediment to all navigation, even the smallest of crafts," wrote M. de Pages in his *Travels Around the World, 1767–1771*. Tobacco and corn were the largest crops, along with cattle production on the farms that were operated by about eighty-five families in the late nineteenth century.[6] It wasn't until the early 1800s that significant development occurred in the parish, with Alexander Fulton laying out the town of Alexandria in 1805 and the parish being created in 1807.

The boundaries of Rapides Parish were quite extensive, from Catahoula to the Sabine River and from Natchitoches to a point in present-day Alexandria.[7] At the time, most of the parish consisted of primeval pine forests on hilly terrain and pine flats, but the lush countryside south and southeast of Alexandria, created by drainage and flooding from the Red River and its tributaries, provided fertile farmland for cotton plantations and other crops.

Visitors to the area west of Bayou Boeuf, with its virgin forests of towering longleaf pines and other trees, called the region the "Great Piney Woods," although the region's values were not thoroughly utilized until late in the nineteenth century, when timber production reached its full potential. "Lands which produced magnolia and cane were considered good; whereas, pine lands were considered worthless," wrote Louisiana botanist Clair A. Brown.[8]

"The planters lived along the rivers and bayous, where slaves worked the flat and fertile fields," according to the *Rapides Parish Louisiana Resources and Facilities*, a survey conducted by the Rapides Parish Planning Board in 1947 that included a history. "The hill lands were little used for planting, although some of the plantations extended into what was known as the Bayou Boeuf pinewoods. It was not until a later day that the virgin pine timber was to meet its destruction."

Even though the impressive longleaf pine is mentioned by Colonel Samuel Henry Lockett, who performed a survey of Rapides Parish in 1869, and though a sawmill is mentioned by Major Amos Stoddard, who traveled up the Red River in 1812, the fertile bayou lands were preferred by Rapides

Parish pioneer landowners, who made fortunes in cotton and slave labor. Lockett credits the "bayou country"—Bayou Rapides, Bayou Boeuf, Bayou Robert and "La Mourie"—with the finest fertile lands. "On either side of the Boeuf and Bayou Robert throughout their length are, or rather were, some of the finest plantations in the state," he reported.

Lockett doesn't spend much time describing the area that now contains Forest Hill—too hilly for cultivating crops, although many small farms existed during his visit in 1869, and too early in the parish's history for sophisticated logging operations. "South of Red river the uplands are the genuine longleaf Pine Hills. Cocodria [*sic*] Bayou, Calcasieu River, and their tributaries all have lands along them which are good and are settled by small farmers."

Again, Northup provided the best snapshot of the Forest Hill area: "The whole country about Red River is low and marshy. The Pine Woods, as they are called, is comparatively upland, with frequent small intervals, however, running through them. This upland is covered with numerous trees—the white oak, the chin-copin, resembling chestnut, but principally the yellow pine. They are of great size, running up sixty feet, and perfectly straight. The woods were full of cattle, very shy and wild, dashing away in herds, with a loud snuff, at our approach."[9]

He described the residence owned by William Prince Ford, a Baptist minister, as located on the "Texas Road," which ran from present-day Alexandria between Lecompte and Forest Hill, through Elmer and Hineston to Burr's Ferry on the Sabine River and on into Texas. "It was two stories high, with a piazza in front. In the rear of it was also a log kitchen, poultry house, corncribs, and several negro cabins. Near the house was a peach orchard, and gardens of orange and pomegranate trees. The space was entirely surrounded by woods, and covered with a carpet of rich, rank verdure. It was a quiet, lonely, pleasant place—literally a green spot in the wilderness."

In addition to the home, Ford owned a sawmill on Indian Creek that Northup determined was about four miles away. Ford's wife owned a large plantation with slaves on Bayou Boeuf.

"Ford's homesite has been confirmed as the Walter Guillory nursery, about ¼ miles east of Forest Hill on the Blue Lake Road," wrote Sue Eakin in her brochure *Northup Trail through Central Louisiana: Beginning at Louisiana State University at Alexandria and Leading through Rapides and Avoyelles Parishes.* "Oak trees, the size of which belies their age, were probably planted about the time that Ford homesteaded 80 acres here in 1836. Ford's house site was at the site of the Guillory residence at the crest of the hill. Hurricane Creek is nearby. The brick kiln with adobe brick remaining on a hillside represents the remains of what must have been another project of Ford. He was pastor of Spring Hill Baptist Church and headmaster of Spring Creek Academy which opened in 1837. The place was on the Texas Road which ran along a ridge in sight of the house site."

During the heyday of plantations, before the Civil War, plantation owners would escape the fever-plagued summers of the alluvial regions of Rapides Parish to the piney woods, where summer homes offered respite from the oppressive heat and continuous waves of yellow fever. One hill country retreat was named Fishville, where teacher Timothy Flint and Judge Henry Adams Bullard owned homes, but most summer residences congregated around Spring Creek near present-day Forest Hill.

"The reason for the uplands retreats was a very serious one," wrote Sue Eakin in *Rapides Parish History: A Sourcebook*. "The lowlands along Red River and the bayous were very unhealthful places to live. A miasma, or ground fog, was credited by some early writers with being poisonous to those who breathed it, and the fevers that swept through the low country, killing so many, seemed to hit residents of the low country hardest."

Northup also wrote of summer residences in the Forest Hill area in *Twelve Years a Slave*, most notably that of William C.C. Martin, proprietor of Sugar Bend Plantation on Bayou Boeuf who owned a summer house next to Ford's. Martin's retreat was located near a cold spring north of Indian Creek, today along Martin Springs Road, named for both the owner and the water source. The small, unpainted house on three or four cleared acres accompanied a barn, and a separate building was used as a kitchen, according to Northup.

"Rich planters, having larges establishments on Bayou Boeuf, are accustomed to spend the warmer season in these woods," he wrote. "Here they find clear water and delightful shades. In fact, these retreats are to the planters of that section of the country what Newport and Saratoga are to the wealthier inhabitants of northern cities."

"In the early days only those compelled by business to do so remained in the alluvial sections during the summer or fever months," according to the 1947 survey *Rapides Parish Louisiana Resources and Facilities*. "Women and children were sent during the summer to quarters in the hills, so they might evade the ever-present fevers that plagued the months of hot weather."

One of the planters was Robert Wilton Bringhurst, a parish surveyor and engineer who spent most of his time in Alexandria, the parish's capital city about eighteen miles to the north. Bringhurst owned a summer residence near Forest Hill and sold the land and gravel bed in April 1907 to the Rock Island Railroad. The "Bringhurst gravel spur" stretched from five miles south of Lecompte on the Red River and Gulf Railroad to the gravel bed, and the gravel removed from Bringhurst's pit was used in ballasting roadbeds of the railroad from Lecompte to Eunice and also for the Colorado Southern Railroad to Eunice.[10]

When the World War II site Camp Claiborne was built on U.S. Highway 165 north of Forest Hill, along with a train station immediately outside its gates, the station depot was named Bringhurst.

Most of these piney woods summer residences are gone, including the names that preceded them. "Nearly every one of these residences is now destroyed, and their former sites can be found only by the clumps of fruit, crepe myrtle bushes, and other exotic shrubs that still struggle for existence in the midst of the vast forest of pines," wrote Eakin in *Rapides Parish History*. "It is a melancholy sight—these mute and ofttimes delicate and beautiful witnesses of a glory now departed forever. They tell a tale of which the beginning and the ending are very different from each other. Wealth, prosperity, luxury are the elements of the introduction to this story: war, ruin, desolation, the burden; poverty the conclusion."

Spring Hill Ward

In the nineteenth century, the Spring Hill Ward was located along the banks of Spring Creek, which originates to the west and south of present-day Forest Hill, cascading into Lake Cocodrie. Spring Hill Ward was long a voting ward for Rapides Parish, and census records suggest that the ward encompassed a large area, including Forest Hill and several miles surrounding the town.

"Spring Hill is the designation of all of Police Jury Ward 4 in Southern Rapides Parish to include Forest Hill to the Allen Parish line, extending east to about Midway, which is in between LeCompte and Forest Hill, extending west to Union Hill," wrote Houston Tracy Jr., a genealogical researcher, on Ancestry.com. "The remainder of Rapides Parish on that side is Ward 6 or Calcasieu Ward."

Lecompte: Plantation Town in Transition positions the Spring Hill community "between White's Landing and Forest Hill on the Old Texas Road," a community used as "a refuge for planters on the bottomland for whom 'the dog days' of late summer were times of terror due to such uncontrollable diseases as infantile paralysis, malaria, and yellow fever."[11] The settlement included the Spring Hill Baptist Church, of which Ford was minister, plus several businesses. Others have pinpointed its location in the neighborhood of present-day Blue Lake Road and Elwood Baptist Church, which coincides with Ford's original homestead, once located on the Texas Road at Hurricane Creek.

The Spring Hill community was the site of Spring Creek Academy, a private boarding school for boys and girls chartered by the legislature in 1837. Ford was president of the school's board of trustees, and Joseph E. Eastburn served as principal, assisted by his wife and four others. Bayou Boeuf plantation owner John Compton, who owned a summer home in the vicinity, was one of its founding members.[12] The legislature insisted that the school be positioned "at some healthy point on Spring Creek in the bayou Boeuf pinewoods" and that "they shall not make the religious tenets of any person a condition of admission as a teacher or student into said Academy."

Incorporators included Robert L. Tanner, Thomas Hughes, Thomas Blackwell Dunham, Joseph Walker, Joseph H. Boone and Hadley P. Roberts, and the first appropriation was $1,500 per year.[13] In its heyday, there were eight hundred students.[14]

There were two buildings on campus, both serving as classrooms and dormitory space, one for girls and one for boys. The school was suspended prior to the Civil War when "Jayhawkers" (roughnecks rebelling from the Confederate draft who stole from residents throughout the region) destroyed the school. The academy never reopened.[15]

In 1903, the Spring Hill School District of Rapides Parish included the communities of Bayou Clear, Blanche, Camp Ground, Forest Hill, Glenmora, Hickory Hill, Indian Creek, Pisgah, Pleasant Hill, Science Hill and Walnut Grove, according to *Historic Hineston*.

Some of the early residents of the Spring Hill area included William Fitz Randolph, William Marshall Butter, Ennis Simpson Duck, Dempsey I. Willis, Burrell Johnson, John Odom, Jacob Gunter, Joseph Chevalier, Frederick Gunter, Robert Graham and his daughter, Emily Graham, who was married to William Marshall Butter by William Randolph, justice of the peace for the Spring Hill Ward.

Today, the actual Spring Creek originates around Roland, northwest of Forest Hill, rolling downstream past Meeker, south of Forest Hill next to the Southern Forest Heritage Museum and Research Center, and into Cocodrie

Lake. The Spring Hill Academy is thought to have existed near the present-day Elwood Baptist Church on Elwood Road, close to its intersection with Butter Cemetery Road in Forest Hill.

BISMARK

Forest Hill became incorporated in 1897; it was a freight station on the Kansas City, Watkins and Gulf Railway, which ran between Lake Charles and Alexandria, and a hub for the healthy sawmill production surrounding the town in the late nineteenth century. Before Forest Hill's official inception, however, there were several named communities in the general vicinity.

To the east of present-day Forest Hill lived William Randolph, a successful landowner and father to Benjamin Hadley Randolph, who later operated a large lumber mill. Although census records on the Randolph family cite their residences as being in the "Spring Hill Ward," next door to the property was a post office named Bismark. Nursery owner Marcia Young now owns the Randolph home and has found remnants of the old post office on her property.

In a biography of Benjamin Randolph by Wanda V. Head in *Biographical and Historical Memoirs of Rapides Parish, Louisiana*, Randolph is mentioned working in the mercantile business at Bismark from 1878 to 1889, when not being able to collect on a debt almost ruined him.[16] Roger Butter in his memoir of Forest Hill, titled *Vittles in the Village* in honor of his mother's Forest Hill restaurant, claimed that Bismark included sawmills and stores. On a late nineteenth-century map, Bismark is marked as being situated west of Cheneyville and slightly to the north and northeast of Babb's Bridge.[17] In the 1890 publication *Rapides Parish: Biographical and Historical Memoirs of Northwest Louisiana*, Bismark is listed as a "post-office village" (and spelled "Bismarck"), along with the neighboring town of Babb's Bridge.

Young, who served as mayor of Forest Hill and researched the town's history, believes that the Bismark name has German origins. So do the editors of the Forest Hill High School reunion book, *FHHS Memories, 1912–1966*. They reported that former Forest Hill postmaster Newton H. Nelson claimed that German chancellor Otto von Bismarck sent surveyors to Louisiana "seeking land for settlements. They named one suggested plot Bismark, and another one a couple of miles west Bringhurst. It is not certain that the first settlers were of German origin. When the railroad was built from Alexandria South, a depot was placed at Bringhurst. The village of Bismark was soon forgotten as a depot was also built at a new location, Forest Hill, just two miles south of Bringhurst."[18]

Roger Butter reports that Von Bismarck of Germany sent surveyors to Rapides Parish with an intention to follow soon after. Bismarck's men arrived and settled where Louisiana Highway 112 exists today, at the site of the old Randolph property. When the railroad depot was established farther west of this site, the town was named Forest Hill.

Some have speculated that Bismark was never used as a town name because of the growing unease between the United States and Germany. "The residents did not want to name the new area Bismark because of the poor blood between the Germans," Butter wrote. "The rail master lived in Lake Charles at the time and often came to the area. It is believed that on one particular trip to Alexandria the rail master took his daughter and stopped on the way and his daughter named it (the new depot) Forest Hill."

It is interesting to note that on a 1912 map that shows the railroad lines between Forest Hill and Lecompte, the stop where Bismark once stood is labeled "Randolph."

BABB'S BRIDGE

Another Rapides Parish community that's no longer in existence is Babb's Bridge, which crossed Spring Creek southwest of Forest Hill near what is now McNary, on the original Louisiana Highway 112 between Lecompte and Sugartown.[19] A post office was established there in 1877, with weekly mail arriving on Wednesdays from Kanomie on Bayou Boeuf, according to the *Louisiana Democrat* newspaper of Alexandria. The town included three mercantiles—Peninger, Dyer and Calhoon—along with two hundred residents in about 1897, according to Winnie Mae Blevins's "History of Glenmora" in the Central Louisiana Genealogical Society's April 1992 periodical.

Martha R. Field, the first newswoman for the *New Orleans Daily Picayune*, wrote a column in 1881 called "Catharine Cole's Letter" in which she opined on women's issues and ventured throughout the state, creating travelogues for her readers. In 1892, she traveled from Vernon Parish into Rapides Parish, heading toward Eunice and stopping at "Babb's Bridge, down in the corner of Rapides parish."

She described Babb's Bridge as a thirty-year-old town on the Kansas City, Watkins and Gulf Railway that was expected to grow as the timber industry expanded:

> *The bridge—Babb's bridge, you know—is an affair of scented pine planks that steeply roofs over a section of a lovely creek, so clear, so pure, that if one cast a newspaper on its shingly bottom I quite believe one could read its pages through the spectacles of the water.*
>
> *It is only one of the typical American villages that has tempted a railway to put a station at its portal, a village where the cottage homes cheerfully hide behind rose gardens, where vegetables thrive in a trim array, and where sweet orchards trail behind the houses, dropping their ripe balls into the long grasses. I was told of an orchard at this place where the pears weigh a pound each. Fancy what a fortune is revealed, like a nugget gleaming out of a gold hill, for some enterprising fruit grower.*
>
> *We put by the ponies at Babb's Bridge and I went by invitation to the schoolhouse to meet the people who came from many miles around to make their gentle welcome. It was worth all the weary days of travel, all the frights and solitary hours to feel the friendly clasp of honest hands, to hear the loyal words of men and women who have the state's good near their hearts.*
>
> *It was nightfall of the second day when I finally left the brawl of Spring Creek and the peaceful homes of Babb's Bridge behind me as I made for the Acadian prairies. And tucked down in my heart, to grow there as a bit of fern in amber, was the four-leaf clover of a phrase that each man and woman had said to me with frank simplicity: "I wish you luck."*
>
> *Out on the prairies, when I looked my last on that golden forest with its golden-hearted people, I said over to myself like a legend, the wish words: "I wish you luck."*

When the railroad arrived in 1890, the town of Babb's Bridge shifted westward and was renamed Glenmora.

Other Ghost Towns

The town of Melder, located near Babb's Bridge and established in about 1840 or 1850, derived its name due to Mr. Melder applying to be postmaster faster than Joseph Chevalier. Chevalier is believed to have been the first person living in the area, and most residents named the town for their pioneer. But Melder owned a store in Chevalier and applied to be postmaster in 1886, thus state officials named the town for him. The town was home to the Chevalier school, established in 1850, and the Central Louisiana Business College (built in 1901), which later burned.

Other communities located around Forest Hill include Midway, located on Louisiana Highway 112 midway between Forest Hill and Lecompte, and Elwood, with the Elwood Baptist Church at its heart, quite possibly the original Spring Creek community. The area of Midway has also been labeled "Holdup," perhaps due to the Red River and Gulf Railroad, which traveled from the Long Leaf sawmill south of Forest Hill to Lecompte.

Many of the families of Forest Hill originated in these outlying towns.

Jayhawkers

During the Civil War, the region was plagued by a group of Confederate draft dodgers known as Jayhawkers, who would confiscate property and harass residents of the piney woods.

"If some of these people were 'ne-er-do-wells,' others were expressing their resentment at fighting what they considered a slaveowners' war, and they felt no call to go to battle for the Confederacy," according to *Lecompte: Plantation Town in Transition*. "They became a gang of men who hid out by day at Jayhawkers Island, only a stone's throw from Spring Creek Academy, and by night they roamed the lowlands destroying all of the plantation culture they could while the planters themselves were mostly gone, either to the war or as refugees in Texas. Deeper yet were the resentments harbored for the planters' airs of superiority towards the hill people and all others not of the elite clan." Many were supported by Union efforts.

Confederate general Alfred Mouton wrote to his forces south of the Red River that Jayhawkers had been spotted from Hineston in Rapides Parish down into Calcasieu Parish and Bayou Teche east of Lafayette—men who were "committing depredations, robberies, and incendiarism, and who are openly violating the Confederate laws, with arms in their hands. Such men can only be considered as outlaws, highwaymen and traitors." He instructed his men to kill all Jayhawkers, including their leaders, found "resisting the operations of the Confederate laws."[20]

Henry Butter hailed from England, arriving in the Forest Hill area in the 1840s. He married Susan Elina O'Neal and built a home in about 1860 with lumber milled on his property. The house still exists on what is now Butter Cemetery Road, and around the property are remnants of the tannery that Henry Butter established, according to descendant Roger Butter.

"One of the most unique stories is of the Jayhawkers, who commandeered the house for storage of their equipment during the Civil War," Roger wrote in his memoir, *Vittles in the Village*. "The Jayhawkers were known to march up and down the front porch of the Butter house demanding food and valuables. On several occasions, the Jayhawkers would march Henry Butter to the tannery and take saddles and other leather items until Henry hid his valuable leather goods in his home attic."

The Grahams were another pioneering Forest Hill family affected by the Jayhawkers. Robert Graham had established a homestead and successful cattle ranch in about 1840 behind the current Mi Tierra Mexican restaurant on U.S. Highway 165. Nearby lived the Gunter and Willis families, who joined the Grahams when Jayhawkers were reported in the area. The group headed to Texas, where Graham family relatives lived. During this time, Robert Graham's son, William Graham, had joined the Confederate army and had not been heard from in some time; the family feared the worst. Unbeknownst to the family, William Graham had been taken prisoner and was jailed at Rock Island, Illinois. After the war, he returned to the Forest Hill area, which was now cleared of the Jayhawkers, and found his family gone. He acquired a mule and followed them to Texas. His reunion with his family was quite emotional, according to family accounts.

Those responsible for removing the Jayhawkers from Rapides Parish included the companies of Major R.E. Wynche and Captain G.W. Smith, as well as David C. Paul, captain of Paul's Rangers. Paul's reputation for dealing harshly with the Jayhawkers followed him after the Civil War, and he was later elected sheriff of Rapides Parish.[21]

Today, maps still pinpoint Jayhawkers Island in Lake Cocodrie southeast of Forest Hill, once a raised mound of land with a spring at its center and live oak trees sporting Spanish moss to conceal those who found refuge there.

OTHER PIONEERS

Many of the early settlers to Forest Hill and the surrounding area have descendants living there today.

Thomas Young and his wife, Juliana Randolph, lived next door to William Randolph, Juliana's father, at Bismark. The Young couple had four children, but both parents died before seeing them into adulthood. Children Walter Francis Young, Josephine Young and Charles Young had moved in with the Randolphs by the 1870 census. Walter Young married Julia Odom (another long-standing family) and became the great-grandfather of Douglas Young, owner of Doug Young Nursery.

Robert Graham had ten children with his wife, Ruth Smith, of Natchitoches. Many of his children married into neighboring families, such as the Dyers, Butters and Merchants. Four of his daughters married sons of Reverend Daniel Hubbard Willis, the grandson of Reverend Joseph Willis, first Baptist preacher to settle in Louisiana west of the Mississippi River. Born a slave in North Carolina, Joseph Willis established the Chicot Baptist Church in 1812, the first Protestant church west of the Mississippi, and then moved to Spring Creek near Glenmora in about 1828. He established the Amiable Baptist Church on September 6, 1828, near Glenmora; the Occupy Baptist Church in 1833 near Pitkin; and the Spring Hill Baptist Church in 1841, near Forest Hill. Reverend Willis is buried at Amiable Cemetery.[22]

Julian Dow Graham helped build the Elwood Baptist Church, and Murphy Gunter purchased the old Graham homestead in 1924. Murphy Gunter was the son of Edward Gunter and the grandson of Jacob Gunter. Upon hearing of the elopement of his daughter, Lucreatia, with Calvin Bass in 1878, Jacob Gunter and his son David Gunter traveled to the house where the couple were staying and killed Calvin Bass. The July 31, 1878 *Louisiana Democrat* sided with the Gunters:

> *It will be remembered that the killing of Bass by the Gunters was under peculiar circumstances, and that Jacob Gunter is an old and respectable citizen of Rapides, and withal a good man, and that both he and his son were tried in Vernon Parish, were found guilty and sentenced for a term of years to the Penitentiary, but made their escape. The trial of the Gunters, at the time, created a great deal of interest, they were zealously and ably defended by Col. R.A. Hunter, a war and lifelong friend of the older Gunter, and bills of exception were filed in their cases, went up to the Supreme Court, and that*

tribunal sustained Col. Hunter's exceptions and sent the case back for a new trial. We mention these facts in justice to the prisoners, the oldest of whom we have favorably known for years, and as this matter has to commence de novo we bespeak in their favor a suspension of public opinion, and let their trial be on its merits and in the interest of pure justice.

In another strange set of circumstances, Edward Gunter, a filling station owner in Forest Hill, was robbed and killed by his nephew, J.D. Gunter, on May 27, 1936.[23]

Beulah Virginia Butter married Ennis Simpson Duck, who bought the old Randolph home after becoming successful in the timber industry. Legend has it that Ennis Duck approached Benjamin Randolph for a job and was turned down, so Ennis swore that he would own the Randolph house one day.

Louisiana Public Service commissioner, nurseryman and longtime Forest Hill resident Clyde Holloway has an office on U.S. Highway 165. The building was once the home of Joseph Wiley Melder and Martha Elvira Squyres on what was considered "Silk Stocking Avenue." Later, their daughter, Jessie Elizabeth Melder, married Winfard Peninger and moved into the house. Jessie Melder Peninger's daughter, Marion, and her husband, George Wiley Davis, later moved into the house after having it remodeled. Today, the building stands as one of the few nineteenth-century homes of Forest Hill. Both the Melders and Peningers owned merchandise stores. Jessie Melder Peninger was part of the first graduating classes of Forest Hill High School in 1912 and returned later to teach.

In the community now known as Midway, Colonel Thomas Jefferson Wells built his summer home, a forest paradise he named Dentley Plantation. In addition to using the property for hunting and other sports, he built a racetrack on which he raced championship horses with other gentlemen of nearby Bayou Boeuf. One of his horses became famous after beating his equine half-brother, an internationally known horse named Lexington, in a race at Metairie Race Track outside New Orleans in 1854. The winning horse of Colonel Wells was named Lecompte; it was this horse that gave the neighboring town its name.[24]

Directly across from the former Dentley Plantation, Sam Stokes and his wife, Mary Ann Musgrove, both natives of central Louisiana, and Mary Ann, the daughter of Reverend Gordon Musgrove (a participant in the famous "Westport Fight" in neighboring Ten Mile Creek), purchased fifty acres of land for fifty dollars. In 1901, Sam Stokes opened a plant nursery, the first in Forest Hill. Little did they realize that they were the beginning of a multimillion-dollar industry.

CHAPTER 2

The Timber Industry

The longleaf pine has long been hailed as premier wood for use in ship construction and the architectural bones of churches, buildings and homes. The English consistently clamored for its wood from American shores and reported on shipment of longleaf as a valuable commodity, and Henry David Thoreau remarked in 1851 that the longleaf pine "is the most esteemed of all pines" in naval architecture, commanding a premium price.[25]

"The long-leaf pine is known to be superior to all the other species in strength and durability," wrote the British Society of Chemical Industry in its 1892 feature on the species. "In tensile strength it is said to approach, and perhaps surpass, cast iron. In cross-breaking strength it rivals the oak, requiring, it is stated, 10,000 lb. pressure per square inch to break it. In stiffness, it is superior to oak by from 50 to 100 per cent."[26]

Early settlers of Rapides Parish revered its virgin forests of short leaf and longleaf pine, among other varieties, but the immensely profitable cotton plantations built with slave labor along Bayou Boeuf were more attractive to landowners moving into the new parish in the nineteenth century. Lack of transportation to move timber from the rural interior was the main concern. Most of the lumber had to be shipped out of the port of New Orleans, which had the first steam-driven sawmill in the nation, so timber had to be moved down the Sabine, Calcasieu and Red Rivers to get to the Crescent City.[27]

There were more than seventy varieties of trees at that time in Louisiana, including 15 billion feet of cypress in the Delta swamps, hardwoods along

Earl Butter (standing with saw) is surrounded by other timber workers in this early twentieth-century photograph. *Southern Forest Heritage Museum.*

the Mississippi River corridor, short leaf pine in the northwest and longleaf pine within five parishes above New Orleans and twelve parishes west of the Mississippi.[28] The state's massive timber resources were ripe for the picking.

One of the first records of lumber production in Rapides Parish came from the eyewitness account of Solomon Northup in *Twelve Years a Slave.* Northup had been kidnapped and sold to William Prince Ford of Rapides Parish and made to work on Ford's mill, located on Indian Creek near the present-day Booker Fowler Fish Hatchery. Ford owned forty acres of virgin timberland in partnership with William Ramsey, and the two built and ran the mill that existed south of the current Indian Creek Recreation Area dam.[29] "Indian Creek, upon which the mills were situated, was a narrow but deep stream emptying into Bayou Boeuf," Northup wrote in his memoirs. "In some places it was not more than twelve feet wide, and much obstructed with trunks of trees."

"Because of the shallow depths of the creeks running through the Great Pine Woods only small mills like Ford's were possible," wrote Meredith Melancon in "William Ford's Lumber Mill" on Acadiana Historical, a website created by the Public History Program at the University of Louisiana–Lafayette. "The larger mills required too much power that the shallow creeks were unable to generate. Upon Northup's arrival at Ford's plantation on Hurricane Creek, he and a few other slaves were assigned to work at the mill. Northup says they spent the summer at the mill piling lumber and chopping logs. It was at the mill that Northup first makes a name for himself in the area."

The Civil War altered Louisiana's economy, and with the beginning of the twentieth century and the advent of new technology and rail transportation to the southern and southwestern piney regions of the parish, a massive new industry was waiting to take hold.

"Before the 20th century it was estimated that the state of Louisiana had 5.9 million acres of longleaf pine timber," wrote T.C. Smith in *The Tale of Three Sawmill Towns: Alco, Meridian and Long Leaf, Louisiana*. "In 1913 it was reported that this acreage represented 120 billion board feet of lumber. Of that amount, about 34.1 billion feet of standing pine trees were located south and west of Red River, representing approximately 2.6 million acres."

Some of the longleaf pines in Rapides Parish grew as high as two hundred feet and at eighteen feet in circumference. Some of these magnificent trees were more than three hundred years old. "They were so thick and tall that the sun was kept from plant life on the ground, therefore, little underbrush existed," wrote Don C. Marler in *Historic Hineston*. "One could see for some distance through the tall stands of timber…It must have been an impressive sight. As beautiful as some of our forests are today they are puny besides these forest of antiquity."

The problem remained in moving the timber from the backwoods to sawmills and then to market. "The only reason Louisiana's debut on the lumbering scene was delayed was lack of transportation, no resources," stated Ed Kerr in *Tales of the Louisiana Forests*. "More than eighty-five percent of the state's land area was in trees. Virgin forests of pines, cypress, and tupelo gum covering all but the sea marshes and southwest prairies lay waiting for the plucking. Louisiana contained more timber (more than one hundred fifty billion feet) than any other state except the Pacific coast states."

Railroads arrived just before the turn of the twentieth century, along with investors ready to take advantage of the vast forest. The Kansas City, Watkins and Gulf Railway was built in the Forest Hill area in about 1892, establishing a depot at Forest Hill that later spawned the town and its name. With the advent of the "Watkins Railway," sawmills quickly popped up within and around the Forest Hill community.

"The timber of Louisiana, a treasure that lay buried for centuries, was suddenly looked upon as a 'pearl of great price,'" Smith wrote. "The majority of the population, who were considered previously as nothing but a blur on the landscape of life, now took on an added significance and they were a force to be reckoned with."[30]

One of the first large sawmill operations was established at Zimmerman, seventeen miles northwest of Alexandria, by J.A. Bentley and E.W. Zimmerman, two Pennsylvanian natives, with the former the builder of Alexandria's Bentley Hotel. As the railroads pushed farther and farther into the rural back roads of Rapides Parish, more mills emerged. In 1893, for example, the Spring Hill Lumber Company Limited completed a large sawmill at Babb's Bridge near Forest Hill, connected by spur to the Kansas City, Watkins and Gulf Railway and boasting of the latest machinery. The sawmill produced twenty-five thousand feet per day, according to the *Times-Picayune* newspaper of New Orleans on February 7, 1893.

Other lumber companies and sawmills located in or near Forest Hill were the Forest Hill Lumber Company Limited at the old Bismark site one mile east from town; the Hurricane Creek Lumber Company, owned by E.E. Richards and his brother, Guy, one mile south of Forest Hill on the Watkins Railroad; Deaux's sawmill, where Sam Poole's Nursery is now located; a mill about one mile north of Midway and operated by George Gaienne; the Peringer-Dixon sawmill; the Keith sawmill; the E.L. Lacroix Lumber Company, east of town, with its modern dry kilns and loading platforms; Branch E. Smith on Mill Creek, a branch of Spring Creek east of town; and the Siess and Ferris Mill, a mile or two above Forest Hill.[31]

"By the end of 1902 there were thirty mills along the Houston, Central Arkansas and Northern or Iron Mountain Railroad (as it was then called) between the Future Great and Monroe," wrote Fredrick Marcel Spletstoser in *Talk of the Town: The Rise of Alexandria, Louisiana, and the Daily Town Talk.*

They collectively cut an average of a million board feet of lumber and filled eighty-five freight cars every day. Moving southward on the Kansas City, Watkins, and Gulf, the settlements of Woodworth, Long Leaf, Forest Hill, and Oakdale more than lived up to their names. The smell of sawdust and the screams of steel blades ripping through freshly hewn logs consistently greeted travelers who passed through those towns on the train. C. Edwin Ball and his sons, V.B. Hayslip, Charles M. Waters, Joseph H. Meeker, Benjamin H. Randolph, Don G. Petty, Ed Rand, J.M. Nugent, Jesse M. Kees, and a host of other men amassed considerable sums of money felling trees.

Rapides Parish native Benjamin H. Randolph inherited land near present-day Forest Hill before the Civil War, growing cotton and other crops in a plantation-

Four timber workers about the turn of the twentieth century. *Southern Forest Heritage Museum.*

style setting. When the timber industry became profitable, he partnered with Joseph Meeker to form the Randolph Meeker Lumber Company. "They grew cotton but they got their money from lumber," said Marcia Young, a Forest Hill nursery owner who now owns the Randolph home and property.

Even though investors and prominent landowners and businessmen created the sawmills and industry, fortunes were made from the timber industry by working men as well. Ennis Simpson Duck spent five years working as a sawyer, the highest-paid worker at a sawmill, for the Forest Hill Lumber Company, beginning in 1890. He married Beulah Virginia Butter in 1892, the daughter of a long-standing Forest Hill family, and in 1895, Duck began working at Long Leaf for seven dollars per day as a sawyer, quite a sum in those days. By 1907, he could afford his own sawmill, opening one in Mississippi before returning to the Forest Hill area to acquire the Flitter Creek mill five miles west of town. After cutting 160 acres of timber from the land within a year, he moved the mill to Roaring Creek.[32]

The largest companies in the Forest Hill area included Hillyer, Deutsch and Edwards west of Glenmora and in Oakdale, mills connected by a private railroad; Louisiana Sawmills southeast of Glenmora; and the W.M. Cady Lumber Company Limited and the McNary Lumber Company, located at and surrounding present-day McNary.[33] The McNary Lumber Company was composed of William M. Cady, president and general manager; James Graham McNary, vice-president and general manager; and Branch E. Smith, secretary and treasurer. The officers of the Cady Lumber Company were Cady, president; Smith, vice-president; and Sam Lisso, secretary and treasurer. Cady was a Louisiana native who cut his teeth at the Louis Werner Sawmill Company in Tioga, Louisiana, and later moved to El Paso, Texas, where he met up with McNary. In 1911, Cady purchased virgin pine forests where the town of McNary now exists and began mill operations in October of that year. Also a Louisiana native, Smith grew up in the timber business. McNary was the only outsider of the establishment, hailing from Indiana and Missouri. He was also college educated; he had made trips abroad and had experience as a teacher of languages and as a newspaperman and financier.[34]

LONG LEAF

Another large sawmill in Rapides Parish—and the closest to Forest Hill—was Long Leaf, originated by timber industry veteran Caleb T. (C.T.) Crowell in 1893 and operated with partner Alexander B. Spencer as the Crowell & Spencer Lumber Company. Long Leaf was one of three sawmills that Crowell established in Rapides and neighboring parishes—the others being Alco and Meridian—and it was centrally located among excellent timberlands, with Barber and Spring Creeks flowing nearby.

"In sawmilling, C.T. always considered first of all the supply of timber," Smith wrote in *The Tale of Three Sawmill Towns*. "Then he made sure that the sawmill location was based on supporting activities such as railroads, and logging camps. Towns were built for each."

After a devastating fire in 1900 destroyed the original mill, the Long Leaf operation moved to a higher location nearby. As the new century dawned, Long Leaf produced seventy-five thousand board feet of lumber each day.[35]

Crowell's son, J. Stamps Crowell, arrived at Long Leaf at age eighteen to run the Crowell & Spencer Lumber Company after the elderly Spencer's health failed.[36] The younger Crowell soon fell into helming the profitable business, which employed hundreds of men in various positions. In 1905, the *Times-Picayune* reported on Stamps Crowell's optimism about the parish's timber industry, although train cars were in short supply to transport timber to market: "Mr. J.S. Crowell, of the Crowell and Spencer Lumber Company,

The logging crew at Long Leaf. *Southern Forest Heritage Museum.*

Ltd., of Long Leaf, La., who was in the city yesterday on a few day's visit, says that the pine lumber business seems better than ever. There has been an improvement in prices, and the outlook for the coming season is very promising. There has been much complaint about car shortage, and is justified. Mr. Crowell says the lumbermen do business with the railroads all the year round and at this time of the year there is always some difficulty in getting enough cars."[37]

Crowell & Spencer established the Red River and Gulf Railroad in 1905 to provide a means for timber to be transported to the Crowell & Spencer mill at Long Leaf and for lumber to reach market. The St. Louis, Iron Mountain and Southern Railroad had tracks beside the Long Leaf mill, but Crowell was subject to the railway's prices and whims. The first track of the Red River and Gulf was laid from Long Leaf toward Lecompte, a distance of about ten miles, snaking through the woods northeast from the mill and then east toward Lecompte, curving just south of the town of Forest Hill. The remaining two and a half miles of track were finished into Lecompte by December 17, 1905, explained Everett Lueck in *A Short History of the Red River and Gulf Railroad of Louisiana, 1905–1953*. The railroad gave Crowell a direct means of moving product to market. "In Lecompte, the Red River and Gulf connected with the Texas and Pacific, the Texas and New Orleans, and the Chicago, Rock Island and Pacific Railroads, giving the mill the competitive outlets that it wanted."

Spurs were created to bring timber to the main line, and branch lines were built to the Crowell mill at Meridian in 1910 and to the mill at Kurthwood in 1920, for a total of seventy-five miles. In addition to transporting timber, passengers utilized the Red River and Gulf Railroad to haul freight, as did other businesses such as turpentine companies and gravel pits. Passengers traveling from Long Leaf to Kurthwood in 1920 would make the trip in three and a half hours. If traveling on a "mixed train," with freight, the journey would average about seven hours.[38]

The Long Leaf mill complex contained just about everything a worker would need. The site included a village of houses, segregated by race, without running water and with outhouses arranged in groups; the commissary, where workers purchased items with company-assigned tokens and later cash; a railroad station and depot; a telephone office; a doctor's office; a barbershop; two Baptists churches, one for each race; a gas station; tennis courts; and a post office that still operates at the site today, among much more. Visitors to Long Leaf had the option to stay at the Long Leaf Hotel and enjoy a meal in the hotel's dining room without having to travel to Forest Hill or Glenmora. When Camp Claiborne was built a few miles north of Forest Hill during World War II, military wives utilized the hotel.

"It was a community unto itself," said Richard Crowell, owner of today's Crowell Lumber Industries and a descendant of C.T. Crowell.

Long Leaf brought timber into the complex via rail, cutting the varieties of tree sizes in the mill, some up to sixty feet tall, said Lueck. The planer mill cut moldings by machine, and the sawdust was utilized to fuel boilers. "This was truly a self-sufficient community," Lueck said. "They didn't waste anything."

Although the Long Leaf community was segregated by race—and the commissary that still exists on the property as the Southern Forest Heritage Museum is a good example, with its lunch counter segregated by a wall of lattice—everyone worked together, said Lueck, the current president of the museum's board. At the mill, for instance, it took two men to cut timber into lumber; a man at the carriage, which moves the log to the band saw; and the "sawyer," who operated the blade that cut the log in four places. "Sometimes you had a white man operating the carriage and a black man at the saw. Or a black man at the carriage and a white man at the saw," explained Lueck. "It didn't matter as long as you got the job

These residents of Long Leaf, seen in front of the Long Leaf Hotel, were labeled "Maxie, Joe, Irene and Mac and Goldberg." *Southern Forest Heritage Museum.*

done." Lueck added that all men were paid the same, depending on the job and not the color of their skin.

Lueck has nothing but praise for J.S. Crowell as an employer, with his research showing that Crowell went above and beyond for his men, paying them thirty cents per hour when the first minimum wage law instituted by the federal government was twenty-five cents. When the company purchased timberland far from the sawmill and town, Crowell built a railroad to transfer the timber back to the mill. Many times, lumber companies would close down sites and move to the site of the timber, Lueck explained, but Crowell didn't want to uproot his people.

Crowell was also one of the few lumber company operators who kept his sawmill open during the Depression, despite the downturn of the economy and the lack of demand for lumber. He cut a regular workweek down to two days so employees would still have an income, but he also cut rents and sold items at the commissary at cost, Lueck explained.

An article in the *Lumber Trade Journal* of March 15, 1917, extolled Crowell's rapport with his employees, as well as the neat and clean appearance of the sawmill and town:

> *The stranger passing by now on Iron Mountain trains secures an impression that the plant of the Crowell & Spencer Lumber Company is something*

new. This impression is due to the fact that the company has made a number of improvements to its property facing the railway, a new store building, ice house, office building and drug store. All nicely painted and handsomely arranged. In addition to this the company always keeps its sawmill building painted and whitewashed, its stocks of lumber are bright as if every stick in the stacks was fresh from a saw, while the sprightly step of employees would indicate in a general way that they are either new on the job or in love with the company. As they have been employed there for years, it is to be understood that the management of the company and the employees are the best of friends. J.S. Crowell, secretary, treasurer and general manager of the company, is one of the best liked men in the lumber business and especially among the men who work for the company.

ACCIDENTS

Cutting timber and working in sawmills was a dangerous occupation, especially in the more rural parishes of Louisiana that lacked quick access to medical care. Also, government regulations protecting workers were nonexistent. On June 11, 1900, the belt of a driving wheel flew loose at the Siess & Company's sawmill near Forest Hill, and the engine "ran away," reported the *Colfax Chronicle* on June 16, 1900. The machinery was torn apart, throwing fragments in all directions, and one piece struck employee Wiley N. Futrell in his face. Futrell never recovered, dying that evening.

At the Keith sawmill near Forest Hill, eighteen-year-old Emanuel Mobley was working the carriage, a piece of machinery in the sawmill that moves logs from their placement into the system along to the saw bank. Suddenly, the carriage started without warning and struck Mobley, throwing him over the roaring saw. Mobley was cut in half just below the waist and died instantly.

In March 1915, William Jordan was thrown from the Cady Lumber Company log train at McNary and fell beneath its wheels, followed by Guy Whittington falling from the log train of the Louisiana Sawmill Company at Glenmora. James Randolph, eldest son of Benjamin H. Randolph, became caught in a belt at the sawmill at Longville and died from the injuries in 1916.

Fires consumed the businesses many times. Sparks flew in mill production at the Hurricane Creek Lumber Company on May 24, 1906, and fell on

Arthur and Jeff Smith work a tree at Long Leaf. *Southern Forest Heritage Museum.*

shavings in the boiler room, starting a blaze that devastated everything but the dry kilns and lumber sheds. Two people were injured and John Hayes killed when a June 6, 1912 thunderstorm blew through McNary, with lightning damaging the Cady Lumber Company's blowpipes and taking out the electric light plant. In 1916, the McNary Lumber Company burned to the ground.

The rapid rise of the timber industry, unhampered by government regulations and sound forestry practices, quickly diminished after the millions of acres of trees had been felled. By the 1920s, much of the region's timber boom was coming to a close, leaving behind waist-high stumps and clear-cut lands where soil erosion began to take hold.

For a brief time, World War I led to the closure of some area timber mills due to the decrease in demand for lumber and the drafting of young men, many of whom worked in the sawmills. "The W.M. Cady Lumber Company's mill at McNary has closed down and has thrown several hundred persons out of employment," reported the August 21, 1914 issue of the *Times-Picayune.* "Suspension is the result of the European situation."

CRIME AND PUNISHMENT

With the new booming timber industry came escalated crime. There were numerous reports of personal assaults and burglaries of train station depots and general merchandise stores in the early twentieth century. Forest Hill also saw a few ghastly murders that made headlines throughout Louisiana.

On January 20, 1895, a thirty-nine-year-old machinist W.C. Roark was watching his wife cook supper after a day of work on the Houston, Central Arkansas and Northern Railway, his head resting on the windowpane with his six-month-old infant in his arms. George W. Swearingen crept up to the window and placed a pistol so close to the window frame that it was powder-burned after he shot Roark at the base of his skull. The ball entered Roark's neck and killed him instantly.

Bradley Shaw testified that Swearingen approached Roark's house at 7:00 p.m., standing about sixteen feet from the window. Roark approached the window from inside his house, which Bradley said was without curtains and contained a lighted lamp. When Roark rested at the window, the child in his arms, Swearingen moved and fired. Swearingen was later arrested carrying a .38-caliber bulldog pistol with one chamber recently fired and shoes that matched the prints found leading from the murder scene to Swearingen's residence. He was brought to jail and subsequent trial in Alexandria.

Roark was a native of Center Point, Tennessee, leaving behind a wife and three children. Swearingen, a blacksmith hailing from Michigan who spent most of his life in Woodville, Texas, had three years earlier stopped a passenger train of the Southern Pacific Railroad in southeastern Texas and forced several passengers off at gunpoint.

The first report claimed that Swearingen had a history with a married woman boarding at Roark's house and that Roark knew of their affair.

The preliminary trial was held on January 18, 1895, but was inconclusive due to lack of evidence. In April, several of Swearingen's friends came forward to vouch for his character, including his brother, Dr. P.G. Swearingen. "This is one of the most important murder trials ever tried in the parish and is attracting a great deal of attention, as the courthouse is crowded," reported the *Times-Picayune* on April 20, 1895. On April 22, 1895, George Swearingen was found guilty.

Ganis B. Keener and his wife, Ellen Carpenter Keener, married in 1890 and lived outside of Forest Hill in a small, simple house without running water. On January 5, 1902, Mr. Keener sent his wife to fetch refreshment at a water hole about 120 yards away. When Ellen Keener returned, her husband stated that he had put the children to sleep and promptly left to visit Mr. Bedgood's to sell him some chickens.

After her husband left the property, Mrs. Keener entered the house and heard one of the children gasping. When she checked on the child, she found her two children—one eighteen months old and an infant twelve days old—dead in their beds with their skulls crushed. She rushed into Forest Hill, insisting that her husband killed the children, and a bevy of Forest Hill's citizens followed her to the house. They found G.B. Keener, still carrying the mark of an axe blade that he claimed his wife inflicted on him when she attempted to murder him in his sleep; he also alleged that his wife had murdered their two children.

Coroner S.H. Rushing held an inquest, and the jury demanded that only Mr. Keener be brought in for murder, claiming that evidence pointed to the husband as the murderer and not the wife. A preliminary hearing on January 31, 1902, ruled that he would remain in prison until his trial, while his wife would be sent to the "poor house on account of her impoverished condition." "He is a fit subject for ready hemp," the *Baton Rouge Advocate* reported on January 9, 1902.

Two months later, still jailed in Alexandria, Keener failed to cut his own throat with a piece of a broken bottle. Although the *Times-Picayune* of March 10, 1902, claimed that he was not "necessarily dangerously hurt," G.B. Keener died four days later on March 14 "from the effects of convulsions which he has been having for months." Keener left a note in his pocket instructing the jailer and sheriff to leave what money he had with him, which was only two dollars, and his pension to "Little Julia Keener, my youngest girl child."

At the Hurricane Creek Lumber Company, mail baskets were kept in the commissary for letters and packages arriving for the mill hands. On April 1, 1908, eighteen-year-old Willie Miller reached into the basket and picked up a postcard addressed to Willie Daniel. He flipped the card over and promptly read the message. Daniel wasn't too pleased with having his mail read. He became enraged, and the two started arguing, which progressed into a fistfight. Twenty-three-year-old J.J. Musgrove witnessed the altercation and attempted to break up the fight.

"Just as he came up Daniel reached behind him and stabbed Musgrove one time in the left side with a pocketknife, the blade penetrating just before the heart," the *Time-Picayune* quoted Deputy Sheriff Mallette in an April 2, 1908 article. "Musgrove died in about thirty minutes after receiving the wound."

The murder by James Mobley of his young wife, Lollie Bedgood Mobley, a native of Oakdale, was called "one of the most deplorable tragedies ever enacted in Alexandria." Mrs. Mobley had earlier that week left her husband, "a well-known citizen of Forest Hill," traveling to Alexandria to live "in a house of ill-fame in the restricted district." On February 14, 1911, James Mobley arrived at the house with their young daughter, "a pretty golden-haired child of about five years of age," according to the February 16, 1911 *State Times* of Baton Rouge. The child was left with an officer who had accompanied Mr. Mobley, the article stated, and Mobley entered a room where his wife was staying and locked the door behind him. The couple allegedly quarreled before witnesses heard several shots ring out.

"Officers were hurriedly summoned, the coroner notified and when they later arrived, the door was forced opened and the couple were lying on the floor, the man with his arms around the woman's neck," the article reported. "The latter had seven bullets in her body, any one of which would have proved fatal."

It appeared that James Mobley had shot his wife five times, emptied the weapon, reloaded the pistol, shot his wife two more times and then killed himself.

THE TOWN THAT MOVED

William M. Cady and his Cady Lumber Company established two mills at McNary, a town twenty-five miles southwest of Alexandria that was chartered in 1913. In the mills' heyday, McNary had a population of nearly three thousand residents, with a church, a school, a post office, a fully staffed hospital, a swimming pool, a depot and a large theater.

In 1923, however, Cady decided to move his operation to Cooley, Arizona, a small American Indian village about 150 miles from Flagstaff and named for Colonel Corridon Cooley, head of the Apache scouts. The Cady Lumber Company purchased the Apache Lumber Company, its Ponderosa Pine timber leases, the accompanying Apache Railway and a sawmill.[39]

But Cady didn't just take the business to Arizona—he took the whole town of McNary with him as well. In January 1924, Cady loaded up trains with Cady employees and all their possessions, plus the logging and sawmill machinery, and moved the entire operation to Cooley, Arizona.

"The tragedy of the timberland was symbolized Monday when the last of McNary, Louisiana, moved away in a twenty-one coach train bound for the new village of McNary, Arizona," wrote Clare D'Artois Leper in *Louisiana Place Names: Popular, Unusual, and Forgotten Stories of Towns, Cities, Plantations, Bayous and Even Some Cemeteries*, quoting a story from the October 1924 *American Forests and Forest Life* magazine. "As the forests became denuded of pines, the employers of the village began looking about for a new site. They found it in Arizona."

Because Cady had built a name for himself at McNary, Louisiana, the town of Cooley was later changed to McNary, Arizona.

"Most of the Central Louisianans who went to Arizona with the Cady Lumber Company stayed in their newfound McNary for at least seven years," said Mrs. N.H. Goff of Alexandria, who was raised in McNary and traveled to Arizona with most of her family. She was quoted in Jim Hammock's *Alexandria Town Talk* newspaper column of July 16, 1967. "They then began drifting to other points in the West, and many returned to Central Louisiana." Goff added that the cold weather may have contributed to their return.

Local Native Americans were hired in Arizona as well, Goff said, but they preferred their native housing and moved out.[40]

The abandonment of its industry and people failed to make McNary, Louisiana, a ghost town, but it struggled to survive. In 1929, its charter became inactive. The community of several hundred residents petitioned the state to have its charter revived, and the town was reestablished in 1965. Today, several of the original mill town houses remain, and remnants of the drying kilns used at both mills can be spotted in the countryside on the outskirts of town.[41]

Not too long after McNary moved to Arizona, John D. Clarke and Charles Linze McNary—no relation to the town—authored the Clarke-McNary Act of 1924 to authorize the government to buy "cut-over" timberland, or land stripped of its trees. Since an enabling act in Louisiana prevented such acquisitions within the state, Alexandria naturalist Caroline Dorman wrote legislation that was passed in Baton Rouge with lumberman Henry Hardtner's assistance to preserve forests in central Louisiana. In 1928, the Kisatchie, Catahoula and Vernon units of the Kisatchie National Forest were established, with more acreage bought at later dates. Dorman was also a good friend of Forest Hill nursery pioneer Sam Stokes.

END OF AN ERA

By the 1930s and 1940s, the heyday of the timber industry had waned. The Long Leaf mill remained, but few others survived. Lands throughout Rapides Parish that had become devoid of timber were purchased by the U.S. government for reforestation efforts.

"On U.S. Highway 165 south of Alexandria, the highway traverses what was once the largest sawmilling area of Rapides Parish," noted the report *Description of Small Towns and Agricultural Communities in Alexandria* by the Louisiana Works Progress Administration. "The mill at Longleaf [*sic*], owned by the Spencer-Crowell Lumber Company is still in operation but there are no longer sawmills at Woodworth, Forest Hill and McNary. Much of the surrounding land has been bought by the U.S. Government and is a part of the Kisatchie Forest. The state forest of six thousand acres is near Woodworth."[42]

The Red River and Gulf Railroad ceased running in 1953, and the Long Leaf mill closed on Valentine's Day 1969, leaving three hundred people without jobs and most of its equipment left on the property wherever the workers halted that day. Train rails have been removed from most of the region, although remnants still exist throughout the Forest Hill woods.

The era of the giant trees came to an end when the forests were cleared. *Southern Forest Heritage Museum.*

The Crowell Sawmill Historic District at Long Leaf was added to the National Register of Historic Places on February 11, 1993, and the Southern Forest Heritage Museum & Research Center opened shortly afterward, in 1994. The museum boasts of having the "most complete collection of steam-powered logging and milling equipment known to exist,"[43] one of the best examples of a sawmill commissary with a segregated lunch counter, the last Clyde rehaul skidder known to exist and two of the last five McGiffert log loaders left in the world today, according to Lueck.

CHAPTER 3

Forest Hill Becomes a Town

Forest Hill was officially dedicated on July 27, 1897, but the town acquired its name much earlier, derived most likely after becoming a depot on the Kansas City, Watkins and Gulf Railway in the midst of the piney wood forests. To the east of present-day Forest Hill was the town and post office of Bismark, but the population followed the railroad, making the depot the center of activity.

"The rail master lived in Lake Charles at the time and often came to the area," Roger Butter related in his memoir, *Vittles in the Village*. "It is believed that on one particular trip to Alexandria the rail master took his daughter and stopped on the way and his daughter named it Forest Hill."

In 1888, the *Lafayette Advertiser* reported on the "citizens of Forest Hill" organizing the Forest Hill Fruit and Vegetable Company and looking to build a canning factory. An 1893 article in the *New Orleans Times-Picayune* reported that the Spring Hill Lumber Company had "completed a large sawmill near Forest Hill Station, on the Kansas City, Watkins and Gulf Railway." The Forest Hill Lumber Company Limited is mentioned in 1894 in the *New Orleans Item*, along with a reporting of the railroad ticket office at Forest Hill being robbed. On September 22, 1895, the Democrats of Forest Hill gathered for a barbecue to hear U.S. Senator Newton C. Blanchard (who went on to become governor of Louisiana) and other politicians who had arrived by train from Alexandria. "Forest Hill is a flourishing village in the hill country," reported the *Times-Picayune*.

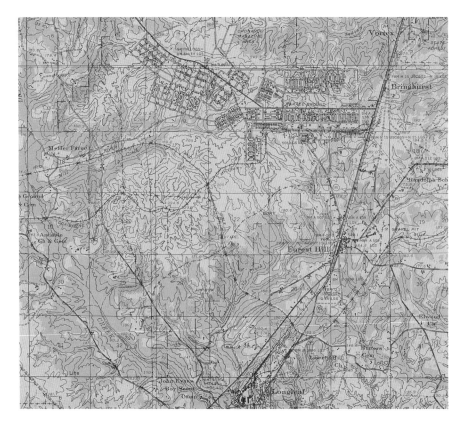

Forest Hill became a town just before the turn of the twentieth century. *Everett Lueck.*

At the turn of the twentieth century, Forest Hill consisted of "eight mercantile establishments, a livery stable, a hotel, a barbershop, a physician, a school and seven sawmills ranging in capacity from eight thousand to forty-five thousand board feet per diem," according to Clare D'Artois Leeper in *Louisiana Places*, adding that "the crossties and wood produced at Forest Hill earn $712,000 per annum."

Some of the early Forest Hill businesses included: Dr. W.H. Dea, drugstore; Mrs. M.L. Moss, dealer in millinery and notions; Jacob Gunter, grocery store; W.W. Malletts and A. Lee Reilly, livery; the Johnson Hotel; D.I. Willis, butcher; W.H. Butter, blacksmith shop; Mrs. J.D. Dunn and Bradley Shaw, cotton gin; and Samuel Johnson, barber.

Forest Hill was home to several general merchandise stores, one-stop shops for many of the town's residents. The Peninger brothers owned a mercantile establishment at Forest Hill that was later purchased by Swift and Sansing in 1923, followed by C.V. Deaux in 1947 and then Dalton and Vertis Chevalier.

"The store was a unique store in the area," wrote Butter. "If you couldn't find what you needed there, it probably was not to be found in Rapides Parish." The same held true for the Murphy Gunter store located on what is now U.S. Highway 165.

Other stores in Forest Hill, according to Butter's memoir and newspaper reports, included the D.R. Johnson store, with Joseph Wiley Melder as manager; R.A. Parrott; the Lyons & Smart mercantile; and Shaw & Melder General Merchandise.

Families lived in town and on farms throughout the area. The more well-to-do lived on Tenth Street, which earned the nickname "Silk Stocking." And those who could afford a telephone received their service from the Melder Forest Hill Telephone Company, run by H.O. Ponder, a former Kansas City, Watkins and Gulf agent who also served in the Louisiana legislature.

In a strange twist of fate, three Forest Hill businessmen broke their right arms all in the same week. In August 1915, barber Sam Johnson, liveryman A. Lee Reiley and farmer E. Mizell accidentally broke their right arms. "It is quite a sad sight to see them all walking down the street to the doctor's office together to have their wounds dressed," reported the *Times-Picayune* of August 14, 1915.

By the turn of the twentieth century, Forest Hill had many schools located throughout the region, including the Smith School, the Dentley School in Midway and a school at Long Leaf, to name a few. The official Rapides Parish schools organized between 1890 and 1900 as the parish population grew.[44]

The Forest Hill School was established between 1900 and 1910 as part of Spring Hill School District No. 5, according to the *South Rapides Chronicle*. In December 1908, a petition was sent to the Rapides Parish School Board asking that a special school district be formed for Forest Hill and a tax raised to build a new school. Both the establishment of the Forest Hill Special School District No. 16 and the tax were approved. In February 1911, citizens of Forest Hill visited Boyce to view the town's new high school building and glean ideas for the building of the Forest Hill school, and later that year, Forest Hill received its own school at a cost of $12,000. The new brick structure that replaced the original wooden school consisted of two stories, with four classrooms on the first floor and five on the second, the principal's office, a sick room, the chemistry lab and a large auditorium with theater seats, balcony and a stage.

The high school officially opened on September 24, 1912, with 127 pupils present. Professor B.F. Lusk served as principal, with five assistants "and a probability of soon adding an instrumental music teacher," according to the September 25, 1912 *Times-Picayune*. The first graduating class of Forest Hill High School was composed of Ellison Gunter, Jessie Melder, Leslie Galligan, Carrie Carnahan, Virginia Daniel, Ruby Dean and Pearl Peninger.

On October 13, 1912, the school was inspected by the Louisiana high school inspector and the parish superintendent, both of whom reported favorably. "Plans are now being made to have the grounds fenced and beautified. Some new residences are being built, and a new store," reported the *Times-Picayune* on October 14, 1912.

By 1916, there were five state-approved high schools in the parish—at Alexandria, Cheneyville, Lecompte, Boyce and Forest Hill.[45] In 1917, the Forest Hill school and the Smith Mill school consolidated, and by 1919, newspaper accounts were reporting the Forest Hill school to be "filled to overflowing with pupils and more teachers are needed. Two transfer buses will be obtained for the benefit of pupils living far from the school. The unusually large number of pupils is explained from the fact that three new gravel pit camps, two turpentine camps and the William Cady Lumber Company camps are nearby, and many families have moved to this section. Negroes employed at the camps are protesting because there is no school to which they can send their children."[46]

Later buildings included the Domestic Science Cottage, built in 1928 for home economic studies; a dining room and kitchen; and first- and second-grade classrooms. For years, students were given an hour to return home for lunch or to enjoy a cold lunch they had brought from home on the school grounds. The first lunchroom at the school was a Camp Claiborne building that was moved from the military base after World War II to the school campus and remodeled for $4,811. Mrs. Eunice Baker Phillips was manager of the lunchroom for nineteen years.

The biggest pride and joy of the early years of Forest Hill High School was the massive gymnasium built by the Gifford-Hill Sand and Gravel Company for use by its company basketball team as well as students. The gym was completed in time for the May 1931 graduation ceremonies, at a cost of $8,055. The gym didn't follow normal measurements for regulation basketball courts, thus giving the home team an advantage. "It was a bigger court than most courts," said Forest Hill native and nurseryman Sam Stokes. "It was a big professional court." Because of this advantage, the Gifford-Hill men's basketball team routinely held winning records. In addition, the high school girls' basketball team, under the coaching of Dorothy Mizell Glass, a World War II Women's Auxiliary Air Force veteran, won three consecutive state championships.

Other schools close to Forest Hill at the turn of the twentieth century included the Pisgah or Dentley School near present-day Paul Cemetery in Midway, where pioneers of the nursery business attended, and the Wildcat School near Tanner Creek on Blue Lake Road, approximately three miles from town. The Wildcat School received its name in 1914 from an unlikely source. "One morning, Mr. Phillips, the principal and most of the student body approached the one-room school with a big surprise," wrote Roger Butter in his memoir. "The door was opened and low and behold to their complete surprise the school had been 'taken over.' They were greeted by a stark, raving, wild wildcat, thus the name Wildcat School."

In 1915, a cold wave bringing ice and sleet killed local farm animals, and when the precipitation melted, it played havoc with roads, bringing business and transportation to a standstill. Later that summer, farmers dealt with an extensive dry spell, which occurred again in 1916, causing crop failures and forest fires. "Drought continues hereabout with no rain for two months," reported the October 11, 1916 *Times-Picayune*. "Forest fires have been raging in this ward of Rapides for the past two weeks and much damage has been done to property and a vast amount of pine timber has been destroyed. The range has been burned off clean and all kinds of stock are suffering for food."

Young men and women from southwest Rapides Parish did their part in World War I, with the first Louisiana resident wounded in the war hailing from Forest Hill. Twenty-two-year-old Chester Johnson, son of D.J. Johnson, the secretary of the board of directors of the high school, was wounded in France in November 1917. Men in the second draft of the war quit their jobs at area sawmills in March 1918 to "help their parents plant the crops before being called into service next April," reported the *Times-Picayune* of March 4, 1918. "It is thought that farm labor will be scarce about cotton-scraping time."

With the growth of the Forest Hill community came a desire to be incorporated. On October 26, 1928, Governor Huey P. Long signed into law the designation of the village of Forest Hill at coordinates "Section 24, Township 1 North, Range 2 West and the north half of Section 25, Township 1 North, Range 3 West in Rapides Parish." The government consisted of a mayor and three-member city council, the first being Mayor Laymen Hendrix Mizell and Councilmen George W. Hollinshed, Leslie E. Reel and Parks W. Sansing (who was also clerk). Their first ordinance on January 18, 1929, was to define and prohibit gambling and provide a penalty for violations.[47]

By the end of the 1920s, with the timber industry waning, gravel pits filled the employment gap, attracting many men. "In the Woodworth-Forest Hill vicinity two gravel companies are in operation," wrote members of the Works Progress Administration in *Description of Small Towns and Agricultural Communities in Alexandria*. "These industries employ many of the men who formerly worked at the sawmills. The number on the payrolls varies with business conditions as the industry is dependent upon building trades."

Small farms found some success with strawberries and sweet potatoes, Irish potatoes in the spring and fall seasons and Satsuma oranges and peaches.

FISH HATCHERY

In the early 1920s, the Louisiana Department of Conservation called for the construction of a statewide fish hatchery to replenish species of game fish in Louisiana streams used for sport fishing. Officials set their sights on a piece of land along Indian Creek three miles from Forest Hill. Dams were constructed on Indian and Burgess Creeks to accommodate the Beechwood Fish Hatchery, "all of them spring-fed and affording an inexhaustible supply of cool, clear water."[48]

"Such a hatchery has long been one of the needed industries of the state, some of the more progressive of American commonwealths having for years maintained such enterprises," wrote the *New Orleans Item* of September 5, 1922. "Louisiana has been somewhat backward in this direction, but having gone deeply into the study of the subject, and exercised unusual care in the selection of site, its project is certain to meet with all the success such efforts have realized in other states." Fish culturist James C. Forsyth, a native of San Marcos, Texas, was the Beechwood Fish Hatchery's first manager.[49]

The first lot of young black bass—a thousand fish ranging from one to three inches long—was dispersed in 1924 to Alexandria attorney T.A.

Carter for his private pond. The fish had been distributed to make room for other species, including sunfish and crappies, claimed Dudley Berwick, conservation commissioner. "Within the next year the conservation department will be able with the six ponds now in operation to supply bass and other game fish in almost any quantity free of charge to any part of the state and the department believes this thoroughly warrants the outlay of $35,000 spent on this project," Berwick said in the May 19, 1924 article of the *Baton Rouge State Times*.

In *Louisiana: A Guide to the State*, by the Works Project Administration, writers described the Beechwood Fish Hatchery in 1941 as a 221-acre tract of land with eight ponds set in groves of trees, with shrubs and flowers planted on the shores of the ponds. "Black and warmouth bass, bream, and perch are propagated and furnished to depleted streams and lakes. The forest and hatchery are wildlife sanctuaries; wild turkeys and quail are fairly common and bear and deer are occasionally seen."

Today, the facility is operated under the auspices of the Louisiana Department of Wildlife and Fisheries and is known as the Booker Fowler Fish Hatchery, producing primarily freshwater sport fish fingerlings. The visitors center at Booker Fowler offers ten thousand gallons of aquaria featuring native Louisiana fish, reptiles, amphibians and crustaceans, in addition to a theater for educational programming and hand-painted murals by local artists Gene Dupuis and Paul Wallace.

Sam Stokes Starts an Industry

There are more than two hundred plant nurseries in and around Forest Hill today, and they all owe their existence to a self-taught man.

Samuel Stokes was born on December 28, 1866, to Samuel Washington Stokes and Kindness Pope of Mississippi. The family moved to central Louisiana in 1869, first settling in Rapides Parish in what would later be Vernon Parish when the boundaries shifted. Young Sam Stokes and his wife, Mary Ann Musgrove, a member of a Rapides Parish pioneering family, moved to the Midway community in 1896, literally halfway between Forest Hill and Lecompte on Highway 112. Their money was meager, but they managed to purchase fifty acres for fifty dollars, a parcel of land with soil a combination of sand and clay. Crops didn't take so well to this piney

Samuel Stokes started the Forest Hill nursery industry in 1901. *Sam Stokes.*

woods land, but the soil allowed for good drainage and easy removal of plants, the perfect habitat for a nursery.

Stokes first grew and grafted fruit trees for his own use, teaching himself planting and propagation techniques. Soon, neighbors began asking for his plants, and Stokes realized that there was a market to be had. He began selling plants to friends and neighbors and then opened a nursery to the public in 1901.

"Samuel Stokes was the first plant nurseryman in the Forest Hill, Louisiana, area," wrote Wilford Perry Stokes in *Stokes, a Family History*. "He was a self-taught, nationally recognized authority on nursery plant propagation."

The tall, blue-eyed man respected all plants, said his daughter, Maude Stokes Athens, in a 1984 *Louisiana Life* magazine article. "He wasn't a… religious man, but he'd sit on the porch when it'd be springtime, and he'd say, 'Now, those leaves, there, they know when to come out. They know when the winter's over.' He could identify all the trees in the woods, even in winter, when they were bare."

Stokes would roam the region's forests and return home, arms covered in flowers, shrubs and other plants ready to be propagated and planted, according to his wife in *Lecompte: Plantation Town in Transition*. "Well, he started raising strawberries, but he couldn't get but fifty cents a gallon for 'em, so he started selling his plants, mostly native growth like holly, live oak, and yaupon," she said. "It was back in the fall of 1900 when we sold our first plants—cape jasmines."

Stokes would travel by train, selling his Rapides Parish plants in Alexandria and New Orleans. He shared his knowledge of Louisiana horticulture with customers, even corresponding with Cammie Henry of Melrose Plantation in Natchitoches, who collected native plants, and conservationist Caroline Dormon, who wrote numerous books on Louisiana trees and plants and helped establish the Kisatchie National Forest in central Louisiana.

"He spent a long time rambling through the woods around here," said Forest Hill resident and nursery owner Marcia Young. "He was an amateur biologist. And Caroline Dorman, who wrote the book [*Wild Flowers of Louisiana*, with the assistance of Stokes], was his pal, and she'd come down or come up from LSU and wander with him in the woods."

Stokes became adept at grafting—a horticultural technique whereby tissue from a plant is inserted onto the rootstock of another and a new plant is produced where the tissues have joined together. Over the years, Stokes produced the first dwarf yaupon holly, a double pink camellia named for his granddaughter Alice Stokes and the propagation of the Governor Mouton camellia from cuttings gleaned from the Mouton family's gardens in Lafayette; Alexandre Mouton was the ninth governor of Louisiana. In front of the Stokes Nursery grew two tung oil trees that he grafted together, forming an arch.

"Papa was always grafting," Athens said. "He'd sit flat down on the floor and graft at night."

Pansies were a big seller for Samuel Stokes and other Forest Hill nursery owners. *Sam Stokes.*

"He's the father of them all," Young said. "There's hardly a state in the union where you can't find a dwarf yaupon."

Nursery plants were grown in the fields when Stokes began his business. Whereas the piney woods soil wasn't ideal for crops, the sandy, porous soil provided a good nesting area for young plants. The piney woods also helped to shelter plants against wind and cold.

"That [soil] was good for azaleas, acid soil," said George Johnson, originator of George Johnson Nursery. "You could grow camellias, hollies; they are acid-loving plants. Mr. Stokes used to go in the woods and pick up seedlings—magnolias and dogwoods, yaupon, American holly. These were all seedlings. He started doing this, selecting this stuff out in the woods. Some of it he planted, and some of it he'd sell bare root. He would plant things in his nursery, but if someone came by wanting to buy them bare root, he'd sell them to them."

For the plants in the fields, customers would arrive at the Stokes Nursery in Midway and choose their plants, and Stokes would dig them up, dip them into a soil mixture and wrap them in moss or burlap. Then they would be ready for the planting when customers reached home.

"Everything was grown in the field, then, like cotton," recalled Hayden Johns Poole Jr. in a 1984 *Louisiana Life* article. "Everybody had

Samuel Stokes loved to experiment with grafting plants. These tung trees at the entrance to his property were grafted together. *Sam Stokes.*

them a little mud hole near the well a little trough like. They'd go in the hills, get sticky red clay off the banks, bring it back and make a thick batter in the mud hole. They'd dip the plant in it coating the roots, lay out a sack and put straw in with the plant and wrap it all up." Later, burlap was used as an outer wrapping for nursery owners selling plants to the public.

Word soon got out about Stokes's nursery and his talent with plants. Customers would travel down from Alexandria and up from Cajun Country. "People would come and eat lunch here because it took so long to get here," said Sam Stokes, great-grandson of Sam Stokes who now owns the nursery with his wife, Donna.

A good part of the business, however, was shipping plants from the Forest Hill depot. Pansies were a huge seller for the Stokes Nursery, and Stokes would steam the soil with a portable boiler to kill grass and other nonessential seeds, then plant the pansy seeds and cover them until they grew. Once pulled from the sand, bundled and boxed, trains would transport the plants all over the southern United States.

Pansies proved a successful plant for Stokes because they could be grown in mass. The plants sold rather cheaply, but Stokes made his money by shipping in bulk. "They were not humongous," Young explained. "You can grow a lot of little bitty plants in a very small amount of sand beds."

Success wasn't easy for Forest Hill residents at the turn of the twentieth century. Lumber mills provided jobs until the forests were cleared, and the piney woods soil wasn't as conducive to farming as the plantation lands to the east along Bayou Boeuf. For Stokes to operate a feasible business, it gave other residents inspiration, and Stokes was willing to share his expertise. He taught Baker Taylor his grafting techniques, for instance; Baker then taught his son, Harvey Taylor. Taylor's nursery opened in the 1920s to grow gardenias, sweet olive, Easter lilies, cherry laurel and Southern magnolia.

Billy Mitchell also caught the fever, starting his nursery in 1923. The Poole brothers, consisting of Murphy Archie Poole and Hayden Johns ("H.J.") Poole Sr., opened a nursery shortly afterward, selling roses and fig trees. They, too, grew plants in the field and removed them bare root to send home with customers, along with offering catalogues and shipment by rail.

By the time of the Depression, there were four large nurseries specializing in ornamental shrubs and trees.

CHAPTER 4

The Great Outdoors

Residents of Forest Hill, McNary and Glenmora sought refuge from Louisiana's hot and humid summers in a dip at the Shady Nook swimming hole, which contained the cool, clear spring waters of Spring Creek. Residents often used the spot—located off present-day U.S. Highway 165 near McNary—for fishing, and organizations such as the Eunice Girl Scouts would travel to Shady Nook to take in the refreshing waters and teach scouts swimming techniques with American Red Cross lifesaving instructors.[50]

Kathryn Brown of Lecompte wrote to "Aunt Jane" of the Dear Jane Letter Club, a column of the *Times-Picayune* of New Orleans, about her recent trip to Shady Nook with her parents and a friend. They left at about sunrise, bringing along "groceries and other things," as Brown wrote of her trip to Shady Nook. They donned bathing suits to enjoy a swim but only stayed in for twenty minutes due to the creek's rather frigid temperature. The group then cooked breakfast over a fire and spent time along the creek's edge before returning home. Later, Lorraine Cooper of Glenmora wrote to the column in 1933 to say, "The swimming hole feels good these hot days. Why don't some of your cousins come to Shady Nook some time? It is a beautiful place and I'm sure you would enjoy the water."

Near Shady Nook, camps for Boy and Girl Scouts were created, with the Boy Scout camp located along Boy Scout Road off U.S. Highway 165, across from Shady Nook.

Cocodrie Lake is a favorite among hunters and fishermen. *Cheré Coen.*

Other favorite swimming holes for Forest Hill residents included the Blue Hole on Indian Creek and the "clear and cold waters" of Tanner Creek, the latter a place where Elwood Baptist Church baptized congregation members, according to longtime resident Roger Butter.

Visitors to Cocodrie Lake expecting something along the lines of a wide-open lake will be surprised to find a dense swamp of tupelo gums, bald cypress and other water-loving trees, with breaks of open water in places. Solomon Northup in *Twelve Years a Slave* escaped his violent plantation master along Bayou Boeuf and traveled through the six-thousand-acre Cocodrie swamp to the home of his original owner, William Prince Ford, who lived on the Texas Road near present-day Forest Hill. Northup called the marshland southeast of Forest Hill the "Great Pacoudrie Swamp," but it's clear that he was referring to Cocodrie Lake.

"It was filled with immense trees—the sycamore, the gum, the cotton wood and cypress, and extends, I am informed, to the shore of the Calcasieu river," Northup wrote. "For thirty or forty miles it is without inhabitants, save wild beasts—the bear, the wild-cat, the tiger, and great slimy reptiles, that are crawling through it everywhere."

Northup encountered both snakes and alligators, he wrote, but created noises to keep both from coming close. One of the most startling scenes to the escaped slave, however, was the ducks that rested on Lake Cocodrie. "After midnight...I came to a halt," he wrote. "Imagination cannot picture the dreariness of the scene. The swamp was resonant with the quacking of innumerable ducks!...My midnight intrusion had awakened the feathered tribes, which seemed to throng the morass in hundreds of thousands, and their garrulous throats poured forth such multitudinous sounds—there was such a fluttering of wings—such sullen plungers in the water all around me—that I was affrighted and appalled. All the fowls of the air, and all the creeping things of the earth appeared to have assembled together in that particular place, for the purpose of filling it with clamor and confusion."[51]

Naturally, because of the ducks and excellent fishing found on Lake Cocodrie, camps were established at water's edge on both sides, including Bennett's Bay Landing, once owned by Lyman Hendrix Mizell, mayor of Forest Hill in the 1920s. Mizell purchased the camp from Mr. Bennett when Bennett became too ill to run the establishment.[52]

"There is excellent fishing in the vicinity during the late spring, summer, and fall, and duck, squirrel, quail, and wild turkey can be hunted in the winter"—this mention of Bennett's Bay Landing comes from the 1941 travelogue *Louisiana: A Guide to the State*, published by the Writers' Program

Left: An old shot of fishermen on Cocodrie Lake. *State Library of Louisiana.*

Below: Indian Creek Recreation Area is a state park north of Forest Hill. *Cheré Coen.*

of the Work Projects Administration. "Northeast of Bennett Bay Landing is another fishing and hunting resort named Blue Lake, where boats and guides are available."

Other popular spots to put in boats and enjoy hunting and fishing at Cocodrie Lake include the Clubhouse Landing, Clark's Landing, Hester's Landing and Johnson's Landing, plus the infamous Jayhawkers Island near where Spring Creek meets the lake, the hiding site for Confederate draft dodgers and renegades.[53]

The Indian Creek Reservoir lies north of Forest Hill, within the Indian Creek Lake and Recreation Area. This state park consists of piney woods with hiking trails, a two-thousand-acre lake and RV and primitive campgrounds. The peaceful lake was created in 1970 by damming Indian Creek farther downstream, to provide irrigation to neighboring agriculture in times of drought. The lake site was developed with assistance by the Louisiana Forestry Commission, the Rapides Parish Police Jury and the Lower West Red River Soil and Water Conservation District, and great fishing is routinely enjoyed at the Indian Creek dam.

Today, there are about one hundred campsites with water and electrical hookups at Indian Creek Recreational Area, three beaches for swimming, bathhouses, a boat launch and seventy-five picnic sites. A covered pavilion provides for groups of up to one hundred people. Visitors can enjoy the park and lake for a day-use fee, which includes use of the boat launch. The Indian Creek Hiking Trail offers a two-and-a-half-mile-long path through a mixed pine-hardwood forest and traverses uplands and minor stream bottoms. Fishing is permitted year-round and in accordance with state fishing regulations. Camping facilities are available on a first-come basis.

CHAPTER 5

The Depression Years

Like towns across America, Forest Hill was hit hard by the Depression of the 1930s. The Great Piney Woods region, in particular, was experiencing a sharp downturn. The booming timber industry had wound down operations in the 1920s, its acres of virgin forests now spent, and few non-farming jobs were to be had outside the region's gravel pit operations.

"They [timber companies] were closing down, and the towns that mushroomed up a few years before in the roar of whirring saws and the lively noises of workers, once again were quiet," wrote the *Rapides Parish Louisiana Resources and Facilities*, a survey conducted by the Rapides Parish Planning Board in 1947. "The hills where the pines had been, showed now only the warts of blackened stumps. The towns, quite suddenly, were gone."[54]

In the parish as a whole, only a few banks reopened after the stock market crash in 1929. Cotton prices declined as well, affecting Rapides's cotton producers in the alluvial plains.[55]

"Hobos were a common sight in the Forest Hill area as the freight train service grew in the South," wrote Roger Butter in *Vittles in the Village*. His mother, Vivian Butter, was quoted in the book as remembering hobos knocking at their kitchen door asking for food. Vivian's mother, Hazel Johnson, fed many of the traveling unfortunates, and her uncle, a janitor at the Forest Hill school, allowed them to sleep inside the school on cold nights. In the morning, the hobos would walk back to the Forest Hill depot and catch a freight train to another town.

Two boys wait for the book mobile outside Forest Hill. *State Library of Louisiana.*

On December 29, 1931, disaster struck Forest Hill. "Fire of undetermined origin last night practically destroyed the entire business district of Forest Hill, La., 35 miles south of here [Alexandria], entailing a loss estimated at $25,000," reported the December 30, 1931 *State Times* of Baton Rouge. "Six buildings were destroyed and three were damaged. The blaze originated in the grocery store of E.W. Mizell and was discovered about 8:45 o'clock. The flames spread from there to the Mizell service station and residence, destroying them. Firemen from Alexandria were summoned, and reached the scene of the fire in time to save other buildings from destruction."

In 1933, President Franklin D. Roosevelt instituted the Civilian Conservation Corps (CCC) to help with the nation's high unemployment rate—then more than 25 percent as a national rate—and as a restoration effort in the nation's infrastructure, primarily building roads and drainage, eradicating soil erosion and working on outdoor projects such as creating state parks and recreation areas. In central Louisiana, the CCC was tasked, among many other jobs, to reforest "cut-over" lands once belonging to timber companies, acres of land cleared of timber and posing erosion problems to the ecosystem. It is estimated that 4.3 million acres of virgin timber were cut during Louisiana's "lumber boom" from 1904 to 1927, leaving the region surrounding Forest Hill devoid of forests and replaced by "a stump-covered wasteland." Many of the timber companies left the cleared lands as is, selling to willing parties or giving them to parishes in lieu of taxes.[56]

The CCC was instituted by Congress and signed into law by President Roosevelt on April 4, 1933, but not without opposition from Louisiana senator Huey P. Long, who called the legislation the "sapling bill" and voiced arguments against planting new trees in Louisiana. He claimed that he would "eat every one of them that comes up in my state."[57]

Support for the program in Louisiana was strong, however, traced to Louisiana's reforestation efforts that began in 1910, when a permanent state conservation commission was established. The Louisiana Division of Forestry was later created in 1916, with forest fire rangers and timber management assistance to small landowners. "Essentially property taxes were lowered in return for the promise of reforestation activities," according to the National Register of Historic Places Database of the Louisiana Office of Cultural Development. "In 1923 contracts were signed to reforest some 141,845 acres. The Division also supervised a boy's forestry club, held summer training courses for rangers, and encouraged property owners to leave seed trees because fully cutover land would not reforest by itself."[58]

One of the ways Louisiana led the nation in reforestation and timber management was the creation of the Alexander State Forest in 1923. "Louisiana, first in reforestation in the South, has now taken the lead by being the first state in the Southern pine belt to establish a state owned public forest," wrote the *Southern Lumberman*. "It stands as an example of what reforestation can accomplish."[59]

Within weeks of the CCC's creation, the new headquarters for District E of the Corps was established at Camp Beauregard, a military camp located in Pineville once used for thousands of soldiers serving in World War I. Plans for a CCC camp in the piney woods would be located in the state forest near Woodworth.[60]

"From 1933 to 1940, a Civilian Conservation Corps (CCC) camp was located on the Forest," noted the Alexander State Forest brochure published by the Louisiana Department of Agriculture and Forestry. "During this period the Corps hand-planted much of the land to pine and constructed the 35 miles of excellent road system still in use today. The CCC enrollees at the State Forest camp, all World War I veterans, also built the log administration building."

Those who joined the CCC program usually remained for six weeks and received food, a place to live, clothing, medical care and thirty dollars per month (or one dollar per day), of which at least twenty-five dollars per month had to be sent to a dependent. Later, enrollment was extended to a maximum of two years. There was to be no discrimination on the part of the government, regardless of segregation issues in the South, but races were nonetheless segregated in southern camps due to lack of government enforcement.[61]

Enrollees for central Louisiana work were examined for employment, and if they passed inspection, they were sent first to Florida and then Camp Beauregard in Pineville. There, they would be conditioned for two to three weeks and then assigned to one of the outlying camps.

Part of the focus of the CCC was to restore lands devastated by timber cutting, so naturally, the U.S. Forest Service and the U.S. Department of Agriculture sponsored most of the CCC camps. In Louisiana, the first camps to be erected were forestry camps within the Kisatchie National Forest and the Alexander State Forest. The camps were assigned reforestation duties and grew trees at the new Kisatchie Stuart Nursery, overseen by Philip C. Wakeley of the Southern Forest Experiment Station.

"Research scientists were assigned to conduct studies at the nursery, and CCC enrollees carried out many of the nursery and field outplanting efforts," noted *The Work of the Civilian Conservation Corps: Pioneering Conservation in Louisiana*. "This collaboration between the CCC and the Forest Service produced data that became the basis for Wakeley's (1954) document *Planting the Southern Pines*, which provided the basic technical knowledge to reforest the South following World War II."

The Stuart Nursery produced 25 million pine seedlings per year that were used by the U.S. Forest Service to reforest areas in several states.[62]

Eight camps were organized in Kisatchie; four state parks were created, and Camp Overton was established at the Alexander State Forest, a prime location of six thousand acres of virgin pine, cut-over lands, bottomlands, uplands and spring-fed wetlands. The 1935 Alexander State Forest Headquarters Building remains, listed on the Louisiana National Register of Historic Places. The 175-foot Woodworth Fire Tower at the state forest headquarters compound is believed to be the tallest fire tower in the world.

Camp Overton at the Alexander State Forest included "an 8,000-acre tract set aside for reforestation and the growing of seedlings for planting in other lumber reclamation areas," according *Louisiana: A Guide to the State*, compiled by the Writers' Program of the Works Progress Administration, another of Roosevelt's job-producing programs. It continued:

> *The forest covers rolling country cut by creek bottoms. Indian Creek, twisting and winding through the woods, alternately loses itself in heavy shade or reflects the sun in open glades. Among the native Louisiana trees here are cypress, three varieties of pine, white ash, sycamore, and black walnut. Although native trees are the chief concern, a constant search is maintained for foreign species that might profitably be grown in the State. About 6,000,000 seedlings are raised annually. The Civilian Conservation Corps has constructed roads, bridges, firebreaks, an observation tower, and camping and picnicking sites. Well-marked roads in the forest lead to three fine recreation areas. Here tables, benches, and*

Pine seedlings grown by the Civilian Conservation Corps in central Louisiana. *State Library of Louisiana.*

fireplaces made of native rock set in a beautiful woodland, afford excellent picnicking facilities. Seven camp sites in all are contemplated. The Administration Building, constructed by CCC men, is composed of native pine logs, peeled and varnished. The large fireplace in the main clubroom is built of stone and mud. Adjacent to the lodge are barracks for the camp worker and an observation tower.[63]

By the end of the Civilian Conservation Corps' nine-year program, eighty-four camps had been developed in Louisiana.[64] "Usually, Louisiana had 25 to 28 camps in operation each year," according to the *Alexandria Daily Town Talk Centennial Edition.* "However, during the peak year, that number more than doubled—from 25 in 1934 to 53 in 1935."

COMPANY 4419 FOREST HILL

Company 4419 Forest Hill began with twenty-five men on July 8, 1935, under the command of Lieutenant George W. May Jr. The men of Company 1490 had left Elizabeth, Louisiana, and marched to Forest Hill to form this new camp, located "a few hundred yards from the paved highway, and approximately twenty miles from Alexandria, in the heart of Louisiana." Later, district headquarters at Camp Beauregard sent a motor convoy of thirteen trucks with tents and supplies for the camp, which grew on August 18, 1935, and was officially established when 175 boys arrived from Gainesville, Florida. On September 2, 1935, construction began on permanent quarters, and within seven days, the camp had barracks, a mess hall, a supply room, a dispensary and a bathhouse, replacing the original tents.[65]

Life at the CCC camps wasn't all work; employees were free at nights and weekends unless work delayed by inclement weather had to be made up. Saturdays usually included dances, movies and sports activities. Camp 4419 at Forest Hill claimed to have the only Code ball course in the state, "as well as the only one operated by any CCC camp," wrote Harry Martinez in his "Sports from the Crow's Nest" column in the *Times-Picayune* of February 16, 1936. The game named for Dr. Edward Code of Chicago was called "poor man's golf," although Martinez likened it to a combination of soccer and golf, "with the former predominating." Balls are moved throughout the course by players' feet, with holes laid at varying distances, from fifty to one hundred yards.

"Perhaps the most attractive feature of the game is that one does not have to be a mere spectator, for as many as a hundred persons can play without a degree of confusion," Martinez explained. "The advantage that this has over baseball and volley ball is obvious. To watch a game is entertainment, but to actually play in the game, that's recreation." Martinez concluded his column by inviting readers to visit the camp to either watch the sport or participate.

On October 24, 1935, the Forest Hill camp held a dance in the Recreation Hall in honor of commanding officers Lieutenant George W. May and Lieutenant E.C. Watson. Locals were invited. "The dance was a great success. The young ladies of Forest Hill and the surrounding communities turned out in force, and the boys and officers spent a most enjoyable evening."[66]

THE NURSERY INDUSTRY EXPANDS

Residents of Forest Hill and surrounding areas continued to farm the piney woods soil, subject to its high acidity and sometimes volatile weather conditions. In many cases, cut-over lands were purchased for farming.

"Truck farming is replacing the timber industry in parts of this area," wrote members of the Works Progress Administration in *Description of Small Towns and Agricultural Communities Surrounding Alexandria.*

> *The growing of truck farming has been given impetus by the owners of the cut-over lands and by the assistance of agricultural agents of railroads in education work and marketing. Groups of colonists from mid-western states have located near Glenmora and Forest Hill during the last decade. Strawberries and sweet potatoes are the principal truck crops but a wide variety of crops are grown. Irish potatoes are shipped in carload lots in both the spring and fall seasons from Glenmora and vicinity. String beans, tomatoes, onions and other vegetables are also shipped. Satsuma orange groves may be seen on some of these tracts and peaches are grown rather extensively. Tung Oil trees are being planted.*

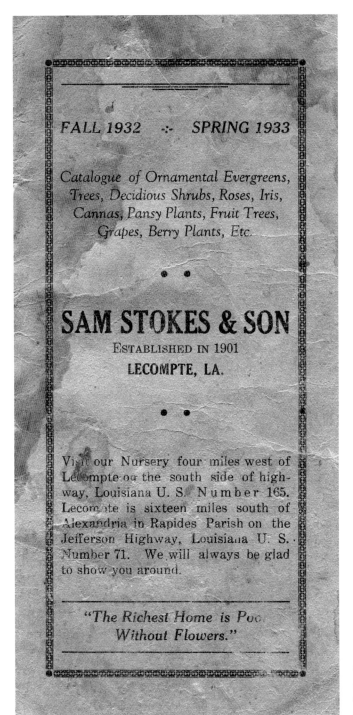

The Sam Stokes & Son catalogue of 1932–33. *Sam Stokes.*

In the 1930s, Sam Stokes & Son Nursery continued its successful catalogue business, shipping pansies and other plants throughout the Southeast from the Forest Hill depot. "Stock is shipped from these nurseries to district markets and an increasing local trade is served," according to *Description of Small Towns and Agricultural Communities in Alexandria*.[67]

The Stokes Nursery's 1932–33 brochure listed a dozen pages of product, including fruit trees, climbing roses, shade trees, hardy palms, deciduous shrubs, conifers, broadleaf evergreens and iris, bulbs and tubers. The nursery also sold the "Stokes Giant Mixture," a collection of flowers "of the largest size and the richest and most varied colors." Plant prices ranged from twenty-five cents to a dollar for a dozen to ten dollars for one thousand. For lots above five hundred, the nursery paid the postage.

"Conscientious effort, careful study and exhaustive tests of Southern trees and plants has made the name of Sam Stokes synonymous with 'high quality' in trees and plants," the brochure noted. "For more than thirty years we have worked to achieve this position, and in the years to come there will be no abatement in our efforts to maintain this reputation. We would like to point out here that we have no agents or dealers through whom we sell. Instances have been called to our attention where unscrupulous dealers have offered inferior stock for sale as genuine Stokes plants."

Samuel Nathanial "Nat" Stokes joined his father in the nursery business, carrying on both the successful business and a true love for plants. Their pansies, advertised as being "unquestionably the world's finest pansies," were planted in Audubon Park and City Park of New Orleans; they were also shipped to many other states. "I believe we're the biggest growers of pansies in the South," Nat Stokes was quoted as saying in *Lecompte: Plantation Town in Transition*.

"My grandparents were doing pretty good back then—not rich by any standard but doing good," said descendant Sam Stokes (great-grandson of the founder), who runs the nursery today with his wife, Donna.

However modest, the nursery business provided enough success for the Stokes family to cause other residents of Forest Hill to take notice. Nat's wife, Milborn Rosalie Strange Stokes, would take their children into Alexandria on Saturdays to shop at the city's department stores or travel to neighboring Lecompte on Friday nights to enjoy the movies.

"Other ladies in the neighborhood got to noticing how nicely dressed they were," said Forest Hill nursery owner Marcia Young. "People looked around and saw people making money, and they got into business to do the same thing. Because that's what happened, when they saw the

Samuel and Mary Ann Stokes. *Sam Stokes.*

Stokes, that's where the Pooles and the Taylors and the Williamses got into business."

"If people see someone doing well in his trade, they get the idea that they could do it too," said George Johnson in a 1975 *Town Talk of Alexandria* newspaper article. "I suppose that's how all of us over here got started in the nursery business."

Nettie Williams started Williams Nursery in 1934 "with an apple box for a rooting bed and a husband who wasn't interested in the business and thought if you didn't start off watering plants, they'd grow without needing it," related Williams's daughter, Martha Lou Vallery, in a 1995 *Louisiana Life* magazine article. "She [Nettie Williams] and the kids did most of the work of that nursery," said Young. "It's always the husbands but remember, behind that husband I don't know of a single wife who didn't work."

The nursery business was anything but easy, said Vallery, who took over Williams Nursery with her husband in 1964. "It was left up to me, as the baby, to climb up and grease the old pulley on the well so we could draw water for the cuttings after dark, rather than hear Daddy fuss. And back then we didn't have electricity—didn't get it until they started building Camp Claiborne in '41. So we'd make cuttings by car light until ten or eleven o'clock at night and get up at five the next morning to set them out by car light."

Everything was done by hand in the early nursery business. Soil was steamed by large machines to rid it of weeds and unwanted plants. Seedlings and seeds were planted in the fields, mainly a root system established in sand and watered by cisterns. The rootstock was then dug up, wrapped in a mud mixture, covered with burlap and sold to the general public.

"We didn't go to college to learn how to do this," Vallery stated in the *Louisiana Life* article. "We went to the College of Hard Knocks. Trial and error. We not only had to learn how to grow them, we had to get out and get people to buy them. But I wouldn't take anything for the experience."

Many of the early nurseries consigned plants to five-and-dime chain stores in Alexandria and other places throughout Louisiana, with business done on a handshake. "Most of the plants sold from 25 cents to 75 cents," said Margie Purkey, daughter of Hayden Johns Poole, in the 1996 *Louisiana Life* article. "We kids would tag the plants for my daddy, write the name and price of each plant at night, to help him. During the Depression, we sold to Kress stores and Morgan and Lindsay, so we weren't hit like a lot of people were. Daddy grew these 50-cent plants, and we did all right."

CHAPTER 6

Camp Claiborne and World War II

When Norma Adams stood before the graduating class of 1942, her salutatorian speech focused less on changing the world as new adults and more on protecting what they held dear. World War II was raging in Europe and the Pacific, but the fight was felt close to home. "We are a class born during the Depression and are come to our seniority at a time of great conflict," Adams told her classmates.[68]

An aerial view of Camp Claiborne.

1. Parker Wiggins and Marjorie Gaunt. 2. Sister Marin, Joe Polancic, and Jo T. Calhoun. 3. Betty Willis and Mildred Browne. 4. "Piccillo" Riggin. 5. Wright Sherrard and Dorothy Jean Gibbs, Parker Wiggins and Marjorie Gaunt, ? and James Sweeney. 6. James Sweeney, Parker Wiggins, and Wright Sherrard. 7, 8, 9. Henry Ford Glass (The Eagle), Dot Mizell (The Bat), Shiek Shehane (The Fly).

Dorothy Mizell, nicknamed "The Bat," trained as a pilot in the Civilian Pilot Training School at the Louisiana State Normal College in Natchitoches. *Louisiana State Normal College yearbook.*

Forest Hill residents did their part in the war effort, with many of the young enlisting into service. Dorothy Mizell, daughter of Gordon Dewey Mizell (who once served as postmaster at Forest Hill), attended the Louisiana State Normal College in Natchitoches (now Northwestern State University), training as a pilot in the Civilian Pilot Training School. Nicknamed "The Bat," Mizell was one of only two women in the course at the time and served as a ferry pilot in the Women's Auxiliary Air Force. Elaine Duck served in the Women Accepted for Volunteer Emergency Service (WAVES), and Julian Dow Graham Jr. served in the army for both World War I and World War II.

Newly ordained Baptist minister Reverend Henry O. Perry worked as a guard during the civilian night shift at nearby Camp Claiborne, in addition to being a substitute rural mail carrier. While his daughter attended Forest Hill High School, Reverend Perry, then a grandfather, went back to school to complete two final years of high school and graduate with the class of 1945. At the commencement ceremony, Reverend Perry gave the baccalaureate sermon.[69]

Forest Hill residents who served included Shelby Williams, Newton H. Nelson, Earl Willis, A.J. Carter, Tommy Delaney and Milford Lamkin. Most of the people involved in the fight for freedom in Rapides Parish, however, were from other states.

LOUISIANA MANEUVERS

Because Camp Beauregard, northeast of Alexandria, served as the District E Headquarters of the Civilian Conservation Corps, the Pineville camp was a natural headquarters for the establishment of military bases in central Louisiana. In 1939, President Roosevelt began a mobilization plan to beef up America's military in the advent of war, and that plan included several bases within the heart of Louisiana.

"People say we were unprepared for World War II, but that's like comparing a NFL team in the off season," said Richard Moran, curator of the Louisiana Maneuvers and Military Museum within present-day Camp Beauregard Army National Guard base. "To bring our army up to speed, the way to do that is by starting a peace time draft and mobilizing the National Guard."

Camp Livingston in the northwest quadrant of Rapides Parish, bordering Grant Parish, and Camp Polk, thirty miles north of Deridder in Beauregard Parish, were established along with Camp Claiborne, located only a few miles north of Forest Hill at the Bringhurst railroad depot, the former site of the Evangeline Civilian Conservation Corps camp. All three military bases—Livingston, Polk and Claiborne—were instituted at the same time, with funds pouring in from the federal government.

"Draftees can be inducted into the National Guard training camps as fast as space to care for them can be provided," Major G.H. Bare, quartermaster of Camp Beauregard, told the *State Times* of Baton Rouge on October 1, 1940. "I know they will be doubled in strength in this area and possibly more than doubled as soon as the camps are completed. The present quota of men for the four camp sites in this area is 64,000."

Camp Evangeline was located on the west side of U.S. Highway 165, about seventeen miles southwest of Alexandria in the Evangeline District of the Kisatchie National Forest. The W. Horace Williams Company of New Orleans began construction of the base in 1940, to provide housing and training facilities for 75,000 men.[70] By the end of 1940, there were 13,300 workmen building the camp, mostly a collection of tents and frame buildings on thousands of piney woods acreage.

"We arrived at the Camp Claiborne site in the fall of 1940," Brigadier General Carlton Smith told his granddaughter, Patricia Lavoner, in 1974 as part of the LSU–Alexandria Oral Records Collection. "The camp area was under a complete construction program. Thousands of workmen from the area were building the temporary housing and utility buildings for the entire camp that was expected to be used early in 1941. The area at that time consisted of 6,195 acres plus a large training and maneuver area extending west to Camp Polk, approximately 40 miles. Much of this area was on a lease basis and was used only as a maneuver and training area. The camp site consisted of a tent area and many more or less permanent tent structures that would last for an unknown period."

Cecil Atkinson remembered when the army came to town, acquiring acreage from area residents and dislocating many, including his family. In his memoir *Camp Claiborne*, he related that mill operator Branch Smith gave his father the house in which they lived since the land where it stood was to become army property. The Atkinson family moved the building up the highway to where his father had purchased forty acres.[71]

Eventually, Camp Evangeline was renamed for William C.C. Claiborne, the governor of the Territory of Orleans and first governor of Louisiana, and officially opened on January 15, 1941. Troops arrived from other parts of the country, mostly the Midwest, and Louisiana boys were sent elsewhere, Moran explained, to give men different experiences in preparation for their time overseas.

"If you were going to fight in the desert, you went to the desert," Moran said. "If you were going to fight in the jungle, you went to Louisiana." The army didn't portray Louisiana's hot and humid climate in such terms, however, preferring to describe the central Louisiana weather as "admirably suited for year-round training as winters are mild and summers are not excessively hot" in its publicity publications.[72]

Even before the Japanese attack on Pearl Harbor and the U.S. entrance into World War II, thousands of soldiers entered Camp Claiborne as well as Camps Polk, Beauregard and Livingston for the Louisiana Maneuvers, training exercises where soldiers branched off into two imaginary countries and fought each other. Camp Claiborne was host to the largest war games in American history in 1941, explained the editors of *The Role of Central Louisiana World Wars I & II*, created by the *Town Talk* newspaper and the Louisiana Maneuvers and Military Museum. "Most notably, the Louisiana Maneuvers were staged in Central Louisiana in 1940 and 1941, and remains the largest peacetime exercise in American military history."

Atkinson passed Camp Claiborne on his way to Forest Hill High School and watched the "trainload of troops" arriving in Forest Hill daily. "At Forest Hill, the small Missouri and Pacific Railroad depot was bursting at the seams with long trains filled with the 34th Infantry Division from North and South Dakota, Minnesota and Iowa. The fifteen to twenty coach troops trains seemed small compared to the double header coal burning monsters that delivered the tanks, trucks, jeeps, and guns by the thousands."

To accommodate the massive troops arriving in Forest Hill, which only contained three hundred residents in 1940,[73] and because the army constantly battered existing thoroughfares, roads had to be improved. In 1941, the army began replacing the eight-mile "winding gravel road" between Lecompte and Forest Hill, "heavily used by the army" as "a short cut between the Baton Rouge-Alexandria highway and Camp Polk," spending between $400,000 and $750,000 on the job.[74]

A railroad depot was established at Bringhurst, a community immediately north of Forest Hill named for Robert Wilton Bringhurst, who owned a summer home in the area at the turn of the twentieth century.

"By the summer of '41 a new railroad spur would be built directly into the camp and a new depot would appear three miles north of Forest Hill at

A railroad depot was established at Bringhurst just north of Forest Hill to accommodate the massive influx of soldiers at Camp Claiborne. *Cheré Coen.*

a settlement called Bringhurst," Atkinson explained in his memoir. "This depot would be used for small freight and personal packages for the soldiers. Mr. Charles Dykes, stationmaster, would take it upon himself to see that every package was delivered to its rightful owner—or at least forwarded to the proper continent once the war picked up."

The first troops to arrive in early 1941 were the 151st Engineer Regiment and the 34th National Guard Infantry Division from Iowa, Minnesota, Wisconsin and North and South Dakota; they were also the first American forces sent to the European Theater of Operations. The 82nd Infantry Division was activated and converted into the 82nd Airborne Division at Camp Claiborne and then split on August 18, 1942, to create the celebrated 101st Airborne Division. The 103rd Infantry was also activated on November 15, 1942.

The camp housed several African American units, including the 761st Tank Battalion, known as the Black Panthers, the latter activated April 1, 1942, at Camp Claiborne with final training at Fort Hood, Texas. The 761st was the first armored African American unit to enter combat; deployed to Europe, it fought at the Battle of the Bulge and landed on Omaha Beach in

France on October 10, 1944.[75] The unit was also among the first to link up with Soviet forces.[76]

The most famous member of the 761st was Second Lieutenant Jackie Roosevelt Robinson, who objected to the Deep South's racial discrimination during his time in Texas and was court-martialed. Robinson left the army with an honorable discharge and went on to cross color lines as the first African American to play in the major leagues of baseball, joining the Brooklyn Dodgers on April 15, 1947.[77]

Because troops at Camp Claiborne were not from the Deep South, the climate, high rates of precipitation and chiggers and other resident pests took the midwesterners by surprise. The *Iowa City Press-Citizen* routinely reported on its boys in a local medical unit at Camp Claiborne, comparing weather notes on May 5, 1941. "Temperatures held to pleasant summerlike levels over Iowa today, but not all Iowans were enjoying the spring. The weather bureau reported that 4.98 inches of rain had fallen at Camp Claiborne, La., in the twenty-four-hour period ended at 6:30 a.m. this morning and that 'it is still raining.'"

"The ground is very hard here," reported Sergeant H. Barteit of Arlington Heights in the *Daily Herald* of Chicago, Illinois. "After digging a few fox holes and slit trenches, it's no picnic. Outside of sleeping on hard ground, killing snakes and scratching insect bites, plus taking care of fat ants, maneuvers aren't so bad."

Corporal Dave G. Vile of Missouri also took aim at Louisiana faults, including "cattle car buses" packed with soldiers on hot summer days traveling to and from Alexandria and Lake Charles. "At Claiborne the climate left something to be desired," he wrote in the *Pampa Daily News* of Pampa, Texas, where he was later stationed. "When the hot season came, day after day, it will never be known how many of us acquired a perpetual case of prickly heat."

Camp Claiborne was the site of the first military railroad to be constructed in the United States. The 711th Railway Operating Battalion and the first troops of the Engineer Unit Training Center (EUTC) created the Claiborne and Polk Military Railroad from Camp Claiborne to Camp Polk. The fifty-mile railway was dedicated on July 11, 1942, with the driving of a golden spike at the halfway mark. Known as the "Green Hornet" and "Old Crime and Punishment," the railway was used for military transportation and also to train soldiers on railway construction, repair and destruction.

The camp grew in the spring of 1942 with the influx of more soldiers and the gearing up of the United States war effort. The addition was called the "West Claiborne Annex," and most of the tents were replaced by "hutments," structures that housed fifteen enlisted men and smaller ones for two officers. Eventually, the two-and-a-half-mile camp, stretching one and a half miles wide, would include more than six hundred frame buildings on 3,100 acres.

"During its brief existence, lasting just over five years, Camp Claiborne saw over a half million men pass through its gates," according to *The Role of Central Louisiana World Wars I & II*. "It was a small town unto itself, complete with its own railroad linking them to nearby Fort Polk."

The army public relations pamphlet, *A Camera Trip through Camp Claiborne*, listed on base a "post office, bank, numerous post exchanges, a chapel for practically every unit the size of a regiment, six well equipped theatres, three guest houses, five service clubs, a large sports arena and commodious bus station, while each company has its own day room. The facilities comprise water works, natural gas, electricity and sewerage."

Famous and not-so-famous entertainers arrived continuously to boost morale, including Gypsy Rose Lee and championship boxer Joe Louis. Military leaders who visited the camp or conducted maneuvers included Lieutenant General George S. Patton, who trained troops at Camp Claiborne in 1941, and General Dwight D. Eisenhower, who visited the camp several times.

Other residents of the camp didn't arrive voluntarily. Italian and German prisoners of war were housed at Camp Claiborne beginning in 1943. Some Germans harvested the region's crops and helped reinforce levees during Red River flooding, and they were housed along the Claiborne-Polk Railroad and southwest of the main gate. In May 1944, several hundred Italian POWs arrived "for the activation of Italian service units," reported the *Camp Claiborne News*.

"It is believed that the utilization of Italian prisoners of war to various duties will help in relieving the army's manpower problem," the newspaper reported. The Italians at Camp Claiborne were housed away from the Germans and used in engineer maintenance companies and petroleum distribution companies with certain privileges, such as payment, camp exchange and theater visits, due to them signing an oath of compliance.

A few POWs managed to escape from Louisiana camps. In 1946, two German POWs—George Schlitzger, twenty, and Josef Schingen, thirty-three—escaped from camp dressed in military apparel and headed toward New Orleans.[78]

BOOM TOWN

One other element that the camp possessed, much to the pleasure of many soldiers and displeasure of camp administration, was Boom Town, a collection of bars, pool halls and stores located outside the camp gates on U.S. Highway 165. Born to accommodate soldiers and their need to blow off steam while off duty, local bar and shop owners made good money during the war years.

"Boom Town was movies, gambling and honky-tonks for servicemen," said Harold Poole Sr., a longtime Forest Hill nursery owner. "The soldiers could get anything they wanted there, including a black eye."

"Boom Town is the camp's midway," noted the public relations office of the army in its *Concerning Claiborne* booklet. "It is located outside of the south gate on what is sometimes referred to as 'Jackass Hill.' It is regulated by a committee of citizens headed by the Mayor of Forest Hill and in cooperation with military authorities. No hard liquor is sold there but beer is available."

In an effort to keep men on base and out of trouble, the booklet offered that "'Off the Reservation' recreation may be found within walking distance of your barracks. Games, amusements, and other types of entertainment are available along with souvenir shops."

Forest Hill residents didn't miss out on the economic boom, offering some of the same pleasure-based establishments seen at Boom Town within its city limits. In its explanation of train stops between Camp Claiborne and Lake Charles or Alexandria, *Concerning Claiborne* described Forest Hill as "little more than a pool hall, drug store and barbershop. The rest of the town's commercial enterprises seem to be liquor stores or honkey-tonks."

"If the soldier could, he would visit the nearby local tavern, the Wigwam that was located along the banks of an old mining pond" in Forest Hill, wrote Roger Butter in *Camp Claiborne: Only the Memories Remain*. The Wigwam later became the Lake Shamaree bar, once frequented by George Jones and Willie Nelson.

Atkinson in his memoir *Camp Claiborne* listed several of Boom Town's businesses, including ones that offered prostitution, although he admitted to changing a few names to protect identities. He named the three-room Duck Inn, with its tarpaper roof connected to "a four-by-six-foot building made of brick and concrete with a steel door on the outside and a large safe on the inside," plus a small barbershop "that looked more like an outhouse." When the health board made its monthly inspection, Atkinson wrote, "It usually closed the Duck Inn down for a few days for a clean up."

Other Boom Town establishments Atkinson named included the Bonnettes' Beer House, "a skinny building stretched straight back from the parking lot. It had no windows in front, only double doors." Sim's Café, a more family establishment, was next door, and Windsor's Place was on the end. Mr. Ford ran Ford's Café, Atkinson recalled, which was "painted white with blue trim and had a large glass window in the front." It remained open twenty-four hours a day.

"The last building on the Boomtown 'strip' was The Trading Post, a large tin building with some sheds in the back," Atkinson noted. "Army goods filled the building—boats, cots, tires, wire, blankets—you name it, they had it. It must have been the original Army Surplus store."

A few Boom Town businesses advertising in the Camp Claiborne newspaper were Bill Phillip's Package Liquor ("1 mile from gate in Forest Hill"); E.W. Mizell's Forest Amusement Club in Forest Hill; Bill's Café, owned by Miss Lillie M. Capperage and Miss Bill Butler, three-fourths of a mile south of the camp; and the Duck Inn, a half mile south, with proprietor Sam Young and taxi service. A photo shot in December 1940 by Marion Post Wolcott of the Office of War Information shows "the new meat market and Portman café."

By 1947, Boom Town had disappeared, and the former Camp Claiborne became part of the Kisatchie National Forest. Today, visitors can still spot remnants of the notorious community by the vague, empty driveways located on U.S. Highway 165 outside the former gates of Camp Claiborne.

LONG LEAF AND D-DAY

Because longleaf pine was so durable and could withstand salt water, lumber from the magnificent trees was sought after during World War II for use in naval operations. One of the most important uses for longleaf pine was in the construction of the Landing Craft, Vehicle, Personnel (LCVP) or "Higgins boat," landing craft used in every major American amphibious operation in the European and Pacific Theaters, including landing on the beaches at Normandy, France, on D-Day on June 6, 1944.[79] These unique boats could transport a platoon of men across water and release them by the bow's movable ramp, which was why they were instrumental in the D-Day invasion; troops moved from England to France across the English Channel and deposited men who were then able to capture the beaches from the Germans.

The boat was designed by Andrew Jackson Higgins of New Orleans, a former timber man who owned the Higgins Lumber and Export Company before moving exclusively into shipbuilding. The movable gate at the boat's bow was the only metal on the craft, the majority of the boat being constructed of plywood. The double keep and the head log, which the metal gate rode on, incorporated longleaf pine for its strength and resistance to rot in salt water, said Everett Lueck, president of the board of the Southern Forest Heritage Museum. And this resilient pine hailed from the Long Leaf sawmill outside Forest Hill.

The trees were carefully chosen for the Higgins boats, which needed twelve feet by twelve feet of heart pine lumber for the boat heads and about seven feet by twelve feet lumber for the keels, as Lueck explained. The Crowell office at the Long Leaf sawmill was burned by an arsonist in 1947, but one letter between Long Leaf owner J.S. Crowell and Andrew Higgins remains, proudly displayed on the museum's commissary wall. The letter references the creation of two thousand Higgins boats using Long Leaf lumber. Lueck believes that many more Higgins boats were constructed, thanks to the Long Leaf mill, although the proof burned in the fire.

"It's highly probable that as many as ten thousand boats were made with timbers cut and milled at Long Leaf," he said. "Without this mill, the war would have lasted two years longer."

Lueck's declaration may sound like an overstatement, but the role of the Higgins boats to the war effort was enormous. General Dwight Eisenhower once said, "Andrew Higgins…is the man who won the war for us…If Higgins had not designed and built those LCVPs, we never could have landed over an open beach. The whole strategy of the war would have been different."[80]

U.S. Marine Corps colonel Joseph H. Alexander said, "The Higgins boats broke the gridlock on the ship-to-shore movement. It is impossible to overstate the tactical advantages this craft gave U.S. amphibious commanders in World War II."[81]

END OF AN ERA

Once victory had been won for the Allies and World War II concluded, Camp Claiborne was deactivated in December 1945; the region returned to its former, quieter livelihoods. "It [Forest Hill] has returned, since the cessation of hostilities, to much the same small local trading center it was before," wrote the 1947 *Rapides Parish Louisiana Resources and Facilities Survey.*

About seven thousand Camp Claiborne buildings were sold or dismantled in 1947, some of which were moved to Forest Hill and exist there today. The acres of land on which thousands of soldiers were stationed was returned to the U.S. Forest Service and reforested. Today, the land is part of the Kisatchie National Forest, some of which is open to the public for camping, hiking, mountain biking and horseback riding. At certain intervals, visitors can see the remains of Camp Claiborne buildings, including a marked spot where the 82nd and 101st Airborne Divisions were created and addressed by Sergeant York under the command of General Omar Bradley on May 7, 1942. York had been a member of the 82nd Infantry Division during World War I.

Other remnants of World War II remain within Forest Hill. Shelby Williams was the first Forest Hill soldier killed in World War II, and the local American Legion Post 256 is named for him.

CHAPTER 7

Growth of the Nursery Industry

Richard J. Polakovich lost his parents at a young age. The Pennsylvania orphan was taken in by a truck farmer who moved to Rapides Parish. To make a living as a young man, Polakovich cut cypress trees in the swamps outside Forest Hill, where he caught a nasty bout of malaria that stayed with him his entire life. He worked as a guard at Camp Claiborne during the war years and walked from his home on Blue Lake Road to the Stokes Nursery and Poole Brothers, where he learned the nursery trade.

Polakovich, like many nursery workers in and around Forest Hill, learned about the growing and cultivation of plants and then brought home the business. Polakovich's employer, Sam Poole, would give Polakovich camellia and azalea cuttings for use in his private endeavors; he then cultivated them on his land. In 1941, with enough plant inventory, Polakovich started his own business: Richard's Nursery.

Many Forest Hill residents after World War II entered the nursery business, while the next generation of nursery owners and workers carried on the family businesses. George Johnson returned home to Forest Hill from World War II service and joined Sam Poole, son of Murphy Poole, and Hayden Johns "H.J." Poole Jr., son of Hayden Johns Poole Sr., in working for the Poole Brothers in 1947 after two years of GI Bill job training.

Harold C. Poole grew up in Midway, halfway between Forest Hill and Lecompte, in a nursery family, entering the business at a young age with his father, Hayden Johns Poole Sr. "My father gave me this property when I was a kid," he said in a 1995 *Louisiana Life* magazine article. "When I was

Sam Poole and Coy Purkey relax in Forest Hill. *George Johnson.*

19, I started a nursery, then I got drafted into the Navy for two years. We had to have a man maintain the place until I came home and started after it again."

Poole married Mary Estelle Carter, who worked as a teacher at the Forest Hill Elementary School. Estelle's job, plus Harold's military service, helped keep the lights on. "When I got out of the service, Korean War, I could hardly pay one man," Harold Poole said. "I eventually paid one man."

The Poole brothers married the Chamberlain sisters, Murphy marrying Odessa Irene Chamberlain, known as "Dessie," and H.J. marrying Bessie Rovilla Chamberlain; both women were part of a family that owned a nursery as well. Johnson, a field operator at Poole Brothers before owning his own nursery, married Murphy Poole's daughter, Vera Lee Poole, and Murphy's son, Samuel Newman Poole Sr., married Wanda Ruth Johnson, Johnson's sister.

"You might say I married into the business," George Johnson told the *Lake Charles American Press*, who spotlighted his nursery in a December 18, 1983 article. "As a boy, I knew every tree in these woods—by the bark and by the leaf but I never dreamed I'd ever be in the growing business."

Like the Stokes Nursery, pansies were a big seller at Poole Brothers, grown in sand beds in slat sheds. "We didn't have hothouses," recalled Vera Poole

The Poole brothers, Hayden and Murphy. *George Johnson.*

Johnson. "We had slat sheds with slats of wood on it, to keep the shade on them. And you had a great cistern on top of that, some kind of a stilt thing way up high."

The plants were pulled from the fields, wrapped and shipped from the Forest Hill depot. "They'd be tons and tons of colors out there," George Johnson said. "Unbelievable." Johnson would haul pansies in the Poole Brothers pickup truck to sites within Louisiana and to neighboring states. "I'd drive all night," he said. "I'd make fifty dollars a trip. That was a lot of money then."

Milton Vallery married into the nursery business when he wed Martha Williams, the daughter of Nettie Williams, who began Williams Nursery in

Steaming the plant beds at Stokes Nursery. *Sam Stokes.*

Opposite: Nathaniel "Nat" Stokes. *Sam Stokes.*

the early 1930s. When Milton returned from service in 1946, he joined his wife working for the family business. "When I came back from the war, my mother-in-law talked me into going into the business," he told the *Alexandria Town Talk* newspaper in 1981. The couple bought out Nettie Williams in 1964, growing a variety of plants, but they were mostly known for their camellias, which they sold all over the country. Their knowledge of camellias earned them the nickname "camellia king and queen" of Forest Hill. "It was at one time even until it went out of business *the* place to buy camellias," said nursery owner Marcia Young.

Robert E. Young of Forest Hill was completely deaf in one ear, so he couldn't enlist during World War II. He worked for Poole Brothers for seventeen dollars per week and then later started his own nursery on purchased tracts of land in receivership from the U.S. government, according to his son, Stanley Young, who owns Forest Hill Nursery Farm.

"About all of them worked for Stokes or Pooles," Young said. "The Pooles were the ones where most of the people got into business. Almost everybody here who's got a nursery worked on somebody else's nursery.

Or they're related. That's how a lot of people got started. It's kind of a family thing."

George Johnson joined Sam Poole and H.J. Poole to buy out Poole Brothers in 1955. When nursery pioneer Sam Stokes died in 1942, his son, Samuel Nathanial "Nat" Stokes, took over the business, along with Nat's wife, Milborn Rosalie Strange Stokes, with help from their children, some of whom would go on to run the business in subsequent years.

Winifred Burnum and O.D. "Buck" Chamberlain established Chamberlain Nursery a few years following the war.

Robert and Edith Young started their own nursery on thirty acres in 1942, building acreage as the years went by. Their children, some of whom would later start their own successful nurseries, worked at the Robert Young Nursery. Stanley Young, for instance, received his grower's permit in 1963. "I was raised on it," he said.

In the postwar years, land was relatively cheap and labor easily available, Young said. Plants—such as azaleas, camellias, hollies and the best-selling wax ligustrum—were grown in the field, dug up and wrapped in burlap, which nursery workers called "B&B," or ball and burlap, according to nursery owner Clyde Holloway. "In the late '50s, early '60s, nearly the entire nursery business was B&B," he said.

Irrigation was done by hand with hoses and movable sprinklers, and sometimes horses were utilized. In lieu of hothouses, plants were placed beneath metal frames with strips of cypress laid on top to allow ambient light through, explained Harold C. Poole. "I didn't have to work hard like they did," Poole said of running a nursery after the postwar years. "They [the generation before him] all worked hard growing up."

One problem that plagued early nurseries was that the large amounts of iron ore in well water would inhibit successful plant growth. Fred Adams, a Forest Hill engineer, developed air wells that pushed air deep into holding ponds and pulled water back up, thereby aerating the system. Aeration not only helps eliminate the iron ore in water but also provides more oxygen to plants.

CANS REVOLUTIONIZE THE BUSINESS

In the early 1960s, nurseries started incorporating metal cans as planters, allowing nursery owners to grow plants in transportable products that used less field space and labor.

"Back when most of this stuff was in the fields and rows, it took a lot of land and a lot of help to be a nurseryman," George Johnson said in a 1983 *Lake Charles American Press* interview. Metal can containers saved nursery owners time, space and money, plus the cans were a lifesaver, Johnson said, when field labor was difficult to obtain. "Everybody started going toward containers," he said. "That was also how the nursery business grew because it didn't take much land to do containers. Off the top of my head, you could grow about twenty to twenty-five thousand cans on one acre of land. In the field, it could take several acres."

Sam Stokes of today's Sam Stokes Nursery remembers the transition from mostly fieldwork to metal can containers happening around the freeze of January 9, 1962.

One great aspect of using metal cans as plant containers was that most of them were free. Metal cans used to store food were a byproduct of the kitchens at Camp Claiborne and other military bases, plus institutions such as schools, prisons and the Central Louisiana State Hospital in Pineville. Nurseries would pick up the used cans, clean them, punch holes in the bottom for drainage, dip them in tar to keep them from rusting and use them for growing young plants.

Johnson would drive to Fort Polk—Camp Claiborne had closed at this point—and pick up two loads of cans per day. Upon his return, he would wash the cans and then dip them in tar. "That was something else, dipping them in tar to keep them from rusting," he said. "Because the fertilizer would eat a rim around the can in a year."

Dean Kellogg of Dean's Nursery also drove to Fort Polk to retrieve cans, said his son, Scott Kellogg. "When my dad started his nursery, we used one gallon metal cans," he said. "Daddy would drive to Fort Polk to get them. He could only haul about 200 to 250 cans at a time. He poked holes in the bottom of them and dipped them in tar to keep them from rusting so quickly. And that's what we planted plants in."

Harold Poole's son, Harold Poole Jr., remembered the runs to gather cans. "We didn't have plastic containers back then, so we'd get old food cans from the prisons in exchange for plants," he said in the 1995 *Louisiana Life* magazine article. "Daddy would give us a penny a container to strip the paper off and punch holes in them."

Stanley Young recalled picking up cans from the local school and tarring them upon reaching home. "All of us had black rings under our fingernails," he said.

One nursery owner drove to the Louisiana State Penitentiary at Angola for cans and accidentally brought home a prisoner, who hid out in his truck, Poole said.

Cans were usually in quart and gallon sizes, plus the "three-egg cans," according to nursery owner Marcia Young, and most of them were free. "We probably had cans on the place for six to seven years," she said. "A lot of times you got cans for nothing, or they cost very little."

Because the metal cans had ridges, it was difficult removing the mature plants. Special can cutters were developed by nursery owners, who split the sides of cans for customers before they left the nurseries.

LINERS

Jonathan Johnetta "J.J." Jeter started working at Poole Brothers Nursery when he was thirteen years old, and Sam Poole was the boss. He continued at the nursery until he graduated from Forest Hill High School in 1969. "That night I enlisted, and I caught the bus and went to Fort Polk the next day," he said. Jeter served sixteen months in Vietnam before returning to Forest Hill, rejoining Sam Poole for thirty-eight years.

In the beginning, Jeter made one dollar an hour at Poole Brothers, with no taxes taken out, so every spring he would have to borrow money to pay the taxman. He began growing liners on the side—a young plant that will be re-potted into a larger container, usually a perennial, ornamental or woody type plant—and used the profits made from selling his liners to pay taxes. In time, Jeter opened his own nursery business, Jeter's Nursery and Liners, and operates it today with his wife, Ann, also a veteran employee of Sam Poole's. "That's how I got involved growing liners on the side," he said, adding that he grew the plants on both his property and Sam Poole's nursery. "He took care of me, and I took care of him."

To make a root cutting, a gardener cuts a twig off a healthy plant, such as a camellia, and dips the base of the cutting in hormones, which helps the new plant develop calluses on the ends and promotes root growth. The cutting then is placed in a soil mixture. "You cut a line with a knife and stick those cuttings in there," George Johnson explained of the process of planting root cuttings. "They'd root right away."

Richard Polakovich received camellia and azalea root cuttings from Sam Poole's nursery, planting them in sand liners in a field when he first started his nursery. "The liner is a root cutting itself," explained Mike Polakovich, who runs the liner nursery today, although also specializing in container plants. Mike remembers sending flower liners by rail from Forest Hill when he was young. "We'd sometimes have that whole platform full of flowers."

Many times, the wives ran the nurseries while the husband held down jobs, Marcia Young explained, and liners were a good business. "Most of

Plant beds at Stokes Nursery. *Sam Stokes.*

that generation were doing it at the time, but the wives were the ones who stayed at home and started it because women could easily do the liners and the sand beds," Young said. "In fact, it's women's work more than it's men's work, because it's little, small work that requires dexterity and it's things that children can do easily."

Pat Brister, who owned Hickory Hill Nursery of Forest Hill, agreed that working liners was a woman's business, employing eleven women full-time in the mid-1990s. "You're dealing with such a small item, and there is so much repetition," she told *Louisiana Life* in a 1995 article. "A man does great with shrubbery and trees. I think it's just the minuteness of this that drives them crazy."

Scott Kellogg, who now owns Scott Kellogg's Nursery, recalled watching his grandmother work liners. "I remember as a small child helping my grandmother, Alpha Kellogg, stick cuttings in sand beds," he said. "After they were rooted we cut, bundled and boxed them. Then she would sell them to local nurseries. I don't know what age I was, but I was probably just in the way. But grandmother never showed it."

WEATHER

Before hothouses, plastic containers and advanced technology arrived to assist nursery owners in dealing with inclement weather, the success of Forest Hill nurseries varied from year to year, subject to rainfall and cold snaps. One of the worst blows to the industry happened on January 9, 1962, when the temperature dropped from eighty degrees to eighteen overnight. The hard freeze remained for several days. Another strong freeze occurred in December that year, followed by two more in January 1963.

Nat Stokes lost 90 percent of his inventory. George Johnson claimed that it was the worst weather he could remember, killing almost all of his plants. "We had troubles then," Johnson recalled in a 1975 *Town Talk* article. "Plants are kinda like people. If the cold comes in easy and the temperature drops gradually, the plants can become accustomed to the weather. It just takes a little adaptation."

In addition to killing plants, hard freezes will break above-ground pipes and pumps, necessary for nursery irrigation.

The back-to-back freezes, ice and snowstorms of early 2014 didn't hamper the Forest Hill nurseries too bad, Ann Jeter said, mostly due to the fact that they received snow more than ice and the freezes didn't last long. "We don't like ice," she said. "We can keep up with snow pretty well, but we don't like ice."

CHANGING OF THE GUARD

By 1966, there were about twenty-five nurseries in the Forest Hill area. It was at this time that Forest Hill first earned the nickname "Nursery Capital of Central Louisiana," although later it would be labeled the nursery capital of the entire state. The town's population clocked in at about five hundred, the city sported a new gas system and streetlights and a water system would follow in 1968. Forest Hill High School received a $50,000 cafeteria, and the recreation program, serviced out of the school park, included three baseball teams sponsored by the town.

"So, with the many nurseries in the area setting the pace economically, with an interested citizenry and a forward looking administration, continued growth for Forest Hill is a certainty," noted the *Louisiana Municipal Review* in its April 1966 issue.

George Johnson's Nursery in 1983. *Burl Vincent, Lake Charles American Press.*

Forest Hill native Clyde Holloway began his nursery in 1968 but maintained his job working for the airlines at Fort Polk until 1981, when he dedicated himself full time to the business. With the death of Nat Stokes in 1962, his sons James Arthur Stokes and Gilbert Rodney Stokes took over the Sam Stokes Nursery. Another son, Samuel Nathanial Stokes Jr., would assist in the business briefly before moving on to the Louisiana Department of Wildlife and Fisheries. Eventually, Rodney Stokes and his wife, Doris Pringle, took over the business.

George Johnson, Sam Poole and Hayden Johns Poole amiably parted ways in 1969, dividing up the land to make things easier for successions when the time came for their children to inherit their businesses. H.J. Poole remained on the original Poole Brothers land, Johnson moved to a tract of land about a mile east on Highway 112 and Sam Poole established a nursery closer to town. Bessie Chamberlain Poole helped manage Midway Nursery with her son, Larry Poole.

By 1975, Johnson was growing about seventy-five varieties of container and field-grown plants, sold throughout the South but with most of his

Previous page and this page: Richard's Nursery. *Mike Palokovich.*

business in Texas, Louisiana and Arkansas. His labor force included about fifteen employees, and his son, Murphy Johnson, helped manage the business. "We grow everything from pine trees to Pampas grass," he told the *Town Talk* newspaper in a 1975 article. "About 40 percent of our plants are sold in cans, about 60 percent from the field. We average about 3,000 plants a shipment."

Jody Polakovich Halbert, the daughter of Richard and Ruby Polakovich, started Halbert's Nursery with her husband, John, in 1972. Michael and Keith Polakovich bought out their father's business, Richard's Nursery, in the 1970s.

Martha Vallery's sister, Doris Morrison, took an interest in the nursery business growing up at Williams Nursery, but from the back end. She studied landscaping and architecture and began designing gardens for homeowners while living in Natchez, Mississippi, including some on the famed Pilgrimage tours. Morrison moved back to Louisiana, working with the Alexandria Downtown Beautification Project in addition to landscaping homes, businesses, plantations and arboretums. "She was *the* landscaper for many years," said Marcia Young. "She landscaped many of the houses in the Garden District [of Alexandria]."

The postwar years provided a nice boost to the nursery business of Forest Hill, building up existing businesses and creating new ones. In 1969, an article in *Town Talk* spotlighting the Central Louisiana Nurserymen's Association claimed that the nursery business of Forest Hill had reached "an annual turnover of about three-quarter of a million dollars a year."

"I have doubled my operation each year so far," George Johnson was quoted as saying in a 1975 *Town Talk* article. "I just try to get as much business as I can and plan my operation around the demand."

Central Louisiana Nurserymen's Association

The Central Louisiana Association of Nurserymen (CLAN) was established in 1955 by twenty-five Forest Hill nurserymen at a time when nursery distributors such as BWI weren't located in town, causing Forest Hill nurseries to purchase supplies individually and at a higher cost. CLAN's original intent was to serve as a cooperative, allowing nursery owners to share in buying and transporting products such as fertilizer and seed into Forest Hill. "The association worked as a co-op," said current president Ann Jeter. "You ordered what you needed and you got it on the truck."

Eugene Duck, chairman of the association in 1969, explained in an article to the *Town Talk* that the bottom line was selling the best merchandise to the public. "We can do this at the best price through volume buying of insecticides, fertilizer and other bulk purchases."

A 1986 brochure, listing sixty nurseries as members, described the organization as a "Limited Agricultural Association" whose purpose was "to promote greater interest in the sale of plants, to achieve common goals and solve common problems, and to set a high standard of business ethics for the nursery industry in Rapides Parish."

CLAN's name was later changed to Central Louisiana Nurserymen's Association (CLNA) because the original abbreviation was offensive to some and caused misinterpretation, Jeter said. "People got the wrong idea when we said we were going to a CLAN meeting."

The organization routinely prints a handy map listing member nurseries in and around Forest Hill and their locations. These can be obtained at Forest Hill City Hall and participating nurseries.

Today, with the more than two hundred nurseries in Forest Hill and surrounding parishes, the Central Louisiana Nurserymen's Association continues to provide networking opportunities for its members and cost-sharing opportunities. Because small nurseries are struggling with an unstable economy, the organization is again discussing cooperative measures, Jeter explained.

Working Together

One of the important reasons for Forest Hill's success, claim many nursery owners, is the town's ability to work together. Nursery owners support other nurseries, buying product from one another and sharing transportation. When problems arise, they come together to help their neighbors.

If hauling plants to a specific location, for instance, nursery owner Clyde Holloway will pick up product for Forest Hill nurseries or bring Forest Hill product to out-of-town customers. "We probably buy at least 100,000 plants from our neighbors to send out in our trucks to send out to our customers," Holloway said. "It's not uncommon for the nurseries around here to buy from each other," added Marcia Young.

When Frank Pittman's greenhouse collapsed in the February 1, 1985 ice storm, he asked his workers for help, as he explained in a 1995 story in *Louisiana Life*. "Word got out, and people started showing up," he said. "They'd come in and work a few hours, then have to get back to their own houses; or they'd send some of their help. Some people had empty greenhouses and offered to move my plant material there. You get so busy working two jobs, you don't get around much to visit neighbors. And you don't know you have friends until you get in a bind and they show up without being asked. This community is like that."

Longtime nursery owner Harold Poole, who has passed the reins on to his children, recalled how nurserymen and women not only helped one another out in the business but also shared all aspects of life. "At the end of the day, nurserymen went fishing," he said. "At the end of the year, they camped out for a few days."

The Murder of Elvin Mizell

One of the biggest events to occur in Forest Hill in the postwar years was the murder of Elvin Mizell.

In April 1949, there was no love lost between Thomas Elvin "Nig" Mizell and Wensley Scott Gunter, the latter the son of Forest Hill town marshal Wensley Crockett "W.C." Gunter. Mizell and Gunter had been opponents in a recent election for town constable that Gunter won; he was later appointed to town marshal. Gunter's home was dynamited "with six sticks of dynamite" on April 24, 1949, a blast so strong that Gunter's daughter lying on a bed within was bounced almost to the ceiling; the mattress alone keeping her from instant death.[82] Naturally, tensions between the two families ran high.

So, when Scott Gunter walked into his home, which housed the telephone exchange, after 8:30 a.m. on April 27 and found Nig Mizell sitting in the front room, things became heated between the two men. Gunter walked into his bedroom, placed his hat on the bed and then returned to the front room, where Mizell asked to speak to him. "He said something about my father and said that if we wanted to live and do well, the whole shebang had better move," Gunter is quoted as saying in an April 29, 1949 article in the *Town Talk* of Alexandria.

Gunter's twelve-gauge shotgun loaded with buckshot was lying beside the door, and when Mizell took a step forward, Gunter lunged for the weapon and shot. It was unclear if Mizell was hit. "By that time my wife was practically between us," Gunter said in the article. "I was on the back with my back towards the kitchen. Then he broke a-loose and my wife either knocked the gun or he knocked the gun and we were spinning so, if I hit him that time, I hit him in the back or in the side."[83]

The two fighting men ended up on the back porch and then moved to the bathroom, where Gunter shot Mizell in the chest, killing him, according to Gunter's statement. Forest Hill native Stanley Young's recollection of the story was that Gunter delivered the fatal shot in the outhouse behind his home.

After the shooting, Gunter came back inside to the telephone board, which was buzzing with a long-distance call. He answered the call at the switchboard but asked the operator for the sheriff's office in Alexandria and was connected. "I told Ray Stuart that I had killed Elvin Mizell," he said.

A state trooper arrived and took Gunter's gun. Gunter kissed his wife goodbye and was promptly arrested and brought to an Alexandria jail. He pleaded guilty to manslaughter, gave a statement to the police that was printed in the *Town Talk* and received a three-year sentence to the Louisiana State Penitentiary at Angola.

Later, the Forest Hill Telephone Company was run by Gordon Dewey Mizell, son of Forest Hill mayor and Rapides Parish justice of the peace Lyman Hendrix Mizell and nephew of Elvin "Nig" Mizell.

CHAPTER 8

The Boom Years

By the 1980s, the Forest Hill nursery business had begun to expand and prosper, primarily due to new technologies and the availability of plastic containers and PVC pipe, which made the growing of plants and irrigation methods easier, more exact and cheaper with less labor. New generations took over existing family businesses or started their own nurseries, while newcomers arrived to join the successful Forest Hill industry.

There may have been a recession in 1980–82, but for Forest Hill, things were blooming. At least that was the pun used in the 1980 *State Times*, which reported area nurseries hitting the one hundred mark, growing at about ten new nurseries per year. "This business has just mushroomed here," nursery owner Hayden Johns Poole was quoted as saying in the article. "There must have been 30 or 40 new nurseries open up in just the last few years alone. I'd have to say that most of the nurseries you see out there (along Highway 112) have opened up in the last couple of years."[84]

The year before, the *Town Talk* newspaper of Alexandria quoted nurseryman Robert Young as claiming that his business was doubling every year. "The total value of ornamental plants grown in the state last year was $30 million, including $10 million added by processing," the article noted.[85]

"The people who are my husband's age, there was kind of a surge there in the early '70s and late '60s, more like the mid-'70s," said nursery owner Marcia Young, who entered the business with her husband, Doug Young, in 1976. "A lot of people from the outside came in. Like Country Pines, Richard Odom. There is a very large group that went into business in the 1970s."

George Johnson at his nursery in 1983. *Burl Vincent, Lake Charles American Press.*

Richard Odom was a farmer of cotton, corn and soybeans, but he searched for a more profitable business, finding it in the Forest Hill nurseries. In 1980, he opened Country Pines Nursery.[86] Evelyn Robbins and O.V. Robbins started Evelyn Robbins Nursery in 1972 after their house burned, said daughter Olivia Nash, who now owns the nursery with her husband, Leonard Nash. "My mother died in 2008, and then we changed the name to Cypress Tree Nursery," she said.

Marcia and Doug Young worked for years at the Louisiana Department of Welfare in Baton Rouge. They adopted a child in 1975, and Marcia took off work for six months, which put the couple behind financially when tax time came around. "We had been talking about how the child loved to fish," Marcia explained. "He was four years old, and we were going to buy a fishing boat with the money we got back from our income tax return, but when we went to pay our income taxes, we had another dependent and I'd been off six months and we owed two thousand to the government. It wasn't fair. We needed a deduction. That's why we went into business."

The couple opened their nursery pointedly on April 15, 1976, located on one slice of Robert Young's land, which was divided out to all of the Young children. Marcia quit her job in 1978 and began working full time at the nursery. The day she arrived in Forest Hill to begin her nursery career was close to her birthday, and retiring from public service was her "birthday present," she said.

Doug Young later retired from the state after thirty years on the job and dedicated himself full time to the nursery in 1997. "What does it take to start a small nursery in a production area such as Forest Hill?" he quipped in *In The Heart of Louisiana: An Illustrated History of Rapides Parish* by Father Chad Partain. "You got it folks! A compact trailer and a wife who will work…and, of course, an acre or two."

Doug Young's brother, Stanley, was in the navy for four years before he returned stateside. He studied farm machinery at the University of Southwestern Louisiana (now the University of Louisiana at Lafayette) and worked at a paper mill in Florida and for oil companies, as well as on his father's nursery. In 1984, he left the oil business and started his own nursery, first in Lecompte and then in the heart of Forest Hill, on Highway 112 where Eco Nursery now stands. In the back was an airport strip that Young used to fly airplanes in and out, he said. Among other plants, he grew ligustrum "by the acres," he said. "I remember the first thing we sold for one dollar. It was a two-year-old wax ligustrum."

Following in his father's footsteps, Mike Polakovich started in the nursery business at age twenty and eventually purchased his father's business, Richard's Nursery. In the late '70s, he grew hardwood trees—oak, cypress, sycamore—for three dollars apiece for area nurseries. When the Louisiana Department of Forestry began selling tree seedlings at a gross discount, Polakovich was forced to change course. "It killed our tree liner business," he said. "They put us out of the tree lining business completely." Polakovich later sold potted liners and rooted cuttings in sand beds and then moved to growing container plants on the thirty acres beside his house.

Pat Brister worked at a construction company, while her husband supervised an asphalt crew. They started Hickory Hill Nursery in 1980 to earn Christmas money, Pat told *Louisiana Life* magazine in 1995. "I had a full-time job, but I thought I could do the greenhouse work on weekends. It took us six months to build that first one—we bent the pipe ourselves. The first year I actually had any plants in there, I didn't sell one red cent of material." Within four years, however, Brister had built two more greenhouses and quit her job.[87]

George Johnson's nursery. *Burl Vincent, Lake Charles American Press.*

Chauncey Nichols learned the business through working at both his parents' nursery and Larry Bates Nursery before starting his own, Chauncey Nichols Nursery. In the end, however, he bought an established nursery so he could grow the business. "I finished high school in 1984, went to work for Larry Bates Nursery for three years," he explained. "I quit and went home to my parents' land and nursery—Garland Nursery—and started my own nursery. It was very small at first—was able to slowly grow the nursery. After three years, I was needing to find my own place. I stopped by Larry Bates, and he told me he would sell me his nursery. I didn't think I could afford it. He told me he could make it work and he did."

Many of the new generations coming up were attending college and receiving related degrees. Harold Poole Jr. earned a degree in horticulture from Louisiana Tech, as did Murphy Johnson, and both eventually took over management or ownership of their parents' respective nurseries.

FOREST HILL'S HISPANIC COMMUNITY

By the late 1970s, as the nurseries grew and the industry expanded, the local labor pool was drying up, especially when it came to field work. Incorporating metal and then plastic containers into the nursery business helped alleviate the problem, but only so much. Even though nursery owner George Johnson discusses the modern changes such as containers in a *Lake Charles American Press* newspaper article in 1983, claiming that he had cut back his employees to twelve, the "back-breaking labor" involved in running a nursery still existed at that time. Johnson listed his duties as tending to six acres of container stock, twenty acres of field stock and six greenhouses with forty thousand seedlings. "There is planting, cutting, spraying, plowing, cleaning and fertilizing, and the almost constant watering," the article noted. "Johnson has three water wells with four-inch pipe. In summer, he waters daily from sun-up to sunset."

Nursery owner Doug Young was the first to consider seasonal workers from Mexico. He had a friend in Many, Louisiana, who had hired Mexican workers for his business, and Young followed his lead, said Doug's wife, Marcia. "We got the first ones," she said.

The first nursery workers hired by Doug Young arrived in 1978 from San Miguel de Allende, Mexico, where many of the current seasonal workers still hail from, said Young. The workers are considered "guest workers," or H-2A temporary agricultural employees with American visas, arriving in Forest Hill for ten months of employment only; they must return to Mexico for two months before they are allowed to come back. The process is highly regulated, said Young, who has a staff member assigned to the government speculations. "Paperwork is humongous," she said.

The federal government regulates the seasonal workers' pay rates and details what the nursery owners must provide them, such as housing and transportation. "And don't think it's cheap just because you're bringing them and they're coming from Mexico," Young explained. "Don't think it's cheap. We don't hire them for five dollars an hour. The government tells you what to pay them, and it's way above minimum wage. We have to provide housing; we have to provide transportation. We have to provide all kinds of things for them. So it's just not that amount that you pay them. It's not cheap. It's because they're reliable workers. It would be way easier for me to go hire somebody here. It'd be tons easier, but you cannot find people to work. It's crazy."

"To work in the United States as a non-citizen worker, you must go through a lengthy process involving lots of paperwork," said Irma Rodriguez, who owns Mi Tierra Restaurante Mexicano. "Nursery owners must do the same."

Today, seasonal workers from Mexico provide the bulk of the nursery business labor, and many nursery owners claim that they have saved the businesses. Murphy Johnson, who now owns George Johnson Nursery, estimated the breakdown to be about 95 percent Hispanic and 5 percent domestic labor. Nursery owner and conservative politician Clyde Holloway admitted that he may have opposed bringing in seasonal workers but found it difficult to find local labor in an industry that demands it. "We're a big labor market here," he said. Nursery owner Sam Stokes added, "Forest Hill would close up tomorrow if they [the seasonal Mexican workers] were gone."

According to a report on the Mexican community of Forest Hill by Dr. William F. Manger of the Louisiana Regional Folklife Program at Northwestern State University in Natchitoches, 12.7 percent of the town's population was of Hispanic origin in 2005, with 90 percent of that figure being Mexican, based on information from the U.S. Census Bureau. Workers of Hispanic origin have increased steadily over the years, growing with the booming nursery industry.[88]

"The Mexican population of Forest Hill has played a substantial role in the growth of the nursery industry within the region," wrote Dr. Manger. "Community members are extremely hard working and, according to nursery owners, are willing to take labor-intensive jobs that most native-born residents will not."

Over the years, several nonnative-born workers have gone on to start their own businesses, carrying on the century-old Forest Hill tradition. Francisco "Poncho" Vargas and Miguel Vargas were brothers who worked for Doug Young in the mid-1980s. They learned the business, saved their money (much like their native counterparts) and opened their own business. "We started in the fall of 1999 with five acres," said Vargas. "We worked for two nurseries before we started working for ourselves, so we learned how to work in nursery."

"Hispanic nurserymen buy plants from one another and start propagating, start selling," Irma Rodriguez said. "They would start with one greenhouse in back and grow plants, then build another one."

Today, Franscico Vargas owns F&M Nursery on Highway 112 and Miguel Vargas owns Vargas Nursery off U.S. Highway 165.

The heart of Forest Hill's Hispanic community lies in the Misión de Nuestra Señora de Guadalupe (or Our Lady of Guadalupe Mission), named for the patron saint of Mexico and part of the St. Martin Parish of the Catholic Diocese of Alexandria. The church began in 1995 to service the growing Hispanic population, helmed by Father Pedro Sierra. According to Dr. Manger, the church interior was built by local Hispanics with donated labor and building materials paid for by fundraisers. The church still raises funds for church upkeep by selling traditional Mexican foods.[89]

"Father Pedro has been a very big piece in this community," explained Rodriguez, who added that non-religious events also occur at the church, such as the Mexican consul offering advice on issues such as healthcare. "He's one of the roots in the tree when it comes to Forest Hill. He's been a very big influence in our community."

Non-Catholic churches in town also appeal to the Hispanic community. For instance, Reverend David Remedios of the Protestant Trinity Christian Center hails from Cuba and his wife, Pastora Yvonne Remedios, from Puerto Rico.

A local market sells Mexican food to the community, and Rodriguez serves up Mexican specialties at Mi Tierra, including her award-winning tamales, which were spotlighted at the 1997 Festival of American Folklife at the Smithsonian Institution in Washington, D.C.

Members of the Hispanic community and native-born nursery workers and owners come to one another's rescue. When Father Sierra first needed a new car, Doug Young offered to help, said Rodriguez, but Sierra asked for assistance with the church instead. "Doug Young cared a lot for our people," Rodriguez said. "I didn't work for him, but I know he cared a lot for the Hispanic community." Recently, when Sierra's car was having troubles and church members looked to purchase him a new car, Marcia Young donated a car to the church.

Another time, when an employee of Doug Young's suffered a stroke, Marcia helped him. "She paid him when he was down," Rodriguez said. "Marcia made sure that man had everything he needed. She's an angel. They're good people."

Nursery Capital of Louisiana

The 1990 article in *CENLA*, the magazine covering central Louisiana, called the nursery industry "Forest Hill's Million Dollar Baby," with more than 50 million plants at the two hundred nurseries of the area at that time. "In fact," the article noted, "the contributions of the Forest Hill area to the nursery business have been so significant that the Louisiana legislature, by official proclamation, has designated Forest Hill as the 'Nursery Capital of Louisiana.'"

Of the two hundred nurseries mentioned in the article, eighty belonged to the Central Louisiana Nurserymen's Association, and most sold stock wholesale, although many retail customers were welcomed to visit, view and buy plants. Much of the nursery stock at that time was sold in Louisiana and within a four-hundred-mile radius of central Louisiana, with occasional shipments veering as far as North Carolina and to major discount garden centers such as Kmart and Walmart. Some nurseries were small operations with "part-time help while others are million dollar operations, stretching out over hundreds of acres and employing up to 30 people."[90]

By the mid-1990s, there were 240 nurseries in Rapides Parish, with 180 in Forest Hill, according to a 1995 *Louisiana Life* article. Wholesale production revenues averaged between $35 million and $40 million annually, the article reported, with about two thousand people "employed in the business of growing and shipping containerized woody ornamentals, bedding and foliage plants all over the South."

The article credited "the explosion of new techniques" as adding to the nursery growers' success, such as computerized irrigation systems, containers replacing field-grown plants and small pots replacing rooting beds in the liner business. "Grow bags, slow-release fertilizer, herbicides and state-of-the-art growing houses all simplify cost-efficient growing for those who can afford—or want—them." These new inventions add to the cost of running a nursery, however. A good potting machine, for instance, could cost between $75,000 and $100,000, the article noted.

One of the largest nursery owners headed to Washington in the 1980s. Clyde Holloway, owner and operator of Holloway's Nursery, was elected to Congress in 1987. He served three terms until 1993, when Louisiana lost a Congressional district due to the reapportionment following the 1990 census, when Louisiana saw a decline in population. A devout conservative, he was the first Republican in the twentieth century to represent the northern section of Louisiana. In October 2006, Holloway was appointed by President George W. Bush as the U.S. Department of Agriculture's state director of the Office of Rural Development, where he served until January 20, 2009. Today, Holloway serves on the Louisiana Public Service Commission.

One of the most successful nurseries in Forest Hill *and* Louisiana was Doug Young Nursery, which, according to the *Louisiana Life* article, was grossing

$3 million per year in the mid-1990s. Doug and Marcia Young owned two businesses at the time—DYN and Young Hollow Nursery—employing twenty-six full-time employees and seasonal workers and selling to accounts that sold to big-box stores such as Lowe's, Home Depot and Walmart. The Youngs specialized in ground covers such as liriope.

"We're in pursuit of profit," Doug Young said in the interview, "and we have a pretty good life. Of course, it's like any other farming activity—you're married to it, and it has its ups and downs. It's a family effort. If it's not a family effort, you usually don't fly."

Forest Hill mayor Woodson McGuffee was also quoted in the article, having nothing but praise for the town of Forest Hill and its booming nursery industry. "It has been a real experience being here, because this town does not have financial problems," McGuffee said. "We own our gas, water and sewer. We have $700,000 in CDs. We use our own money to get things done. And the people here are very independent, financially strong and real hard workers."

FOREST HILL CULTIVARS

Forest Hill nurseries have been responsible for creating several new cultivars, plants carefully maintained through propagation.

Sam Stokes is responsible for several camellia cultivars, including the Alice Stokes camellia, named for his granddaughter; a dwarf yaupon holly; and a rare pink dogwood from the central Louisiana woods. One of Stokes's most beautiful camellia cultivars was the Governor Mouton camellia, established from cuttings taken from the long-standing Lafayette family gardens, according to *History of the Central Louisiana Association of Nurserymen*.[91] Mouton served as the state's governor from 1843 to 1846, and his sugar plantation, named Ile Copal, included a camellia that grew to "such grand height and strength that, at one time, a chain was fastened into it for attachment of a hitching post for horses," according to a January 21, 1959 article in the *State Times*.

The Robert Young Nursery, with assistance from the LSU Cooperative Extension Service, introduced the "Bonnie" dogwood, which grew wild in Union Parish. For three years, Young propagated the tree, one sturdy enough for the Gulf Coast region and its warm climate. "This is a tree capable of withstanding the hot, humid climate and producing especially large white

The Governor Mouton camellia. *American Camellia Society and Massee Lane Gardens.*

flowers measuring four and a half to five inches across," wrote Garden Editor Rachel Daniel in her April 8, 1979 column in the *Times-Picayune* of New Orleans.

Doug Young Nursery created the Samantha liriope, sporting a pink flower.

Richard Polakovich of Richard's Nursery developed the Richard's boxwood from a seedling at Herbert LaFleur's nursery; three boxwoods have been patterned by Polakovich.

The Williams Nursery cultivated the Williams boxwood.

Martha Lou Valley of Williams Nursery earned the title of camellia expert after years of camellia cultivation. Her nickname became "Camellia Lady."

CHAPTER 9

Taking Over Education

L ike in most of the South, if not the nation, education resources were not equally distributed between black and white citizens in Louisiana. The U.S. Supreme Court decision of *Brown v. the Board of Education of Topeka* changed everything in 1954, declaring the segregation of American schools illegal.

In the region surrounding Forest Hill, schools followed the race line. Lincoln Williams Elementary was 93 percent African American in 1980, and Forest Hill Elementary and Poland High School were overwhelmingly white. Forest Hill had been integrated in 1971 and had 26 black students enrolled in 1980 out of 311 students total.[92]

Integration throughout the parish was overdue, said Judge Edwin Hunter Jr. of the Fifth District Appeals Court. "When the *Brown* decision came almost everybody among my close friends thought the decision was long overdue…and I among them," he told Sue Lyles Eakin in *Rapides Parish: An Illustrated History*.[93]

The process to correct segregation became much more complicated and heated among parents, teachers and administrators. In Forest Hill, students from kindergarten through high school went to school locally until 1966, when the high school was consolidated into Rapides High School in Lecompte. For the small agricultural town, having a local school was important to Forest Hill residents, even if only for elementary students.

"The school, however, was more than an educational institution; it was the community center and the heart of Forest Hill," wrote Eakin. "Boy

Scouts and Girl Scouts, adult singing groups and ball teams, short courses, family reunions, fundraisers for such benefactors as St. Jude's Hospital for children, political rallies and parents groups met at the school. At election time, it became the voting place for the precinct."

It was because of this close-knit association between a small town and its school that things blew up when Judge Nauman Scott handed down the July 3, 1980 order to bus students to Lecompte. The order demanded that the predominately white Poland High School and Forest Hill Elementary be closed, along with the predominately black Lincoln Williams Elementary in Cheneyville. Students from all three schools would merge into the Lecompte schools to "achieve a satisfactory racial balance at Lecompte."[94]

Forest Hill and Poland residents objected to the closure, but no one was more vocal than nursery owner Clyde Holloway. Holloway's father believed in three things—school, church and work, Holloway said. Growing up along Blue Lake Road, Clyde walked six miles to attend football practice at Forest Hill High, returning home without a flashlight, having to dodge cows and other farm animals in the dark.

Having a school close to home was important to both the children and the community, he insisted. "I'm opposed to the busing concept," he told the *Alexandria Town Talk* newspaper in July 14, 1980, when he announced that he would run for the U.S. House of Representatives against incumbent Representative Gillis Long. "I'm not opposed to integration. I was in the beginning, but like most Americans I've grown to accept it."

Holloway's young children attended the Forest Hill school and would be bused to Lecompte under the order. The Holloways' only alternative was to send them to private school in Alexandria. Holloway insisted then, and does today, that most African Americans in the parish agreed with him that busing wasn't the answer. He stated in the article that the black students at Forest Hill equaled the amount of black children in the area and that if the judge wanted to bus more black students into Forest Hill, he would welcome it.

"I think the School Board and the people should be able to run their schools without intervention by a federal judge and when I go to Washington I will be doing everything to prevent this," he told the *Town Talk* in 1980.

Despite Forest Hill parents' opposition, the court order stood, and when the time came for the Forest Hill students to be bused into Lecompte, parents opened the local school on September 9, 1980, and took it over. Teachers and parents were poised to run the school on their own. The event received nationwide attention, with an Associated Press photo of the American flag being raised upside down at half-mast in the Forest Hill schoolyard plastered on newspapers everywhere. "Walter Cronkite ended his show with, 'That's the way it is in Forest Hill, Louisiana,'" Holloway recalled.

Judge Scott wasn't too pleased with the takeover. After two weeks of parents teaching children in the school, with Holloway acting as principal, Scott inflicted fines of $300 per day to Holloway, $200 per day to teachers and $100 per day to others remaining on school property. At this point, the "squatters" removed themselves, but they left behind a sign at the front gate: "Unjustly seized and closed by Justice Dept."[95]

Classes composed of seventy-four students, five of whom were black, were then moved to three Forest Hill churches: Forest Hill Baptist Church, Pisgah Baptist and Elwood Baptist.[96] Holloway stepped down as principal, and Estelle Poole, a long-standing teacher in Forest Hill, was appointed. Several Rapides Parish teachers joined the school.[97]

Forest Hill resident Jay Chevalier, who made his mark when his song "The Ballad of Earl K. Long" sold thousands of copies, planned a concert to support the school. His latest song was titled "Holloway's Heroes."

The K-8 school was called the Forest Hill Neighborhood School, with both teachers with educational backgrounds and "volunteer teachers," such as parents. By May 1981, the school housed "174 students, down from their high point of 191," wrote Raymond L. Daye in the May 14, 1981 *Town Talk* column "Daye in School." The kindergarten and grades four through six were at Forest Hill Baptist, seventh and eighth grades at Elwood and first through third at Pisgah.

"Mrs. Poole said she is not worried about next year or the effect a year out of public school will have on the children," Daye wrote. "She is confident the children's education has not suffered and said the school organizers have been careful to prepare their eighth graders for graduation to ninth grade at Rapides High School in Lecompte."

The following summer, the parish school reopened for a rally in the gymnasium, with Ninth Judicial District judge Richard E. Lee present. "This gymnasium should be enshrined as the last American freedom shrine," Lee told the crowd assembled at the school for the first time since they held a Christmas program in the gym. He likened the takeover of the Forest Hill school to that of the Revolutionary battle of Lexington and Concord, known as the "shot heard 'round the world": "Another shot was heard around the world today. It was fired by the people of Forest Hill," he concluded.[98]

Later, the school became Forest Hill Academy, offering classes from kindergarten through twelfth grade. To accommodate the school, parents and teachers first built portables at Forest Hill Baptist and then constructed the building where Forest Hill Elementary is now and moved the portables there. Parents and Holloway built the cafeteria and gym, he said. "We built it all ourselves," Holloway said. "The only thing we hired to build was the drop-in ceiling. Everything else we built."

Holloway owned the Louisiana Speedway racetrack, purchasing it after a Woodstock-like concert was held there and Holloway felt the musical event was the wrong element for the town. "I just bought it for my kids to have a nice place to grow up in," he said. When Forest Hill Academy opened, the school's football team played at the racetrack, with students utilizing the bleachers he brought over from Louisiana College.

"Had Forest Hill been a settlement of affluent people, this would not have been so remarkable, but the contributions represented incredible sacrifices," Eakin wrote in *Rapides Parish: An Illustrated History*.

In May 1988, the first group of Forest Hill Academy students graduated from high school. "I think it shows that the school is not just a temporary thing," Principal Glenn Williams was quoted as saying in a May 20, 1988 *Town Talk* article. "We're not a protest school anymore." The 15 graduates were from a student body of 193.

Holloway continued to support the private Forest Hill Academy, which his children attended, helping keep the school afloat with his own finances and through fundraisers such as the Louisiana Nursery Festival, he said. Meanwhile, parents continued to fight to reopen Forest Hill Elementary, a long legal battle that lasted for years. The school later reopened as a Rapides Parish school and is the town's elementary school today, serving close to four hundred students from pre-kindergarten through sixth grade—58 percent of students today are white, 38 percent Hispanic, 2 percent Asian and 2 percent American Indian, with 1 percent African American.[99] The cafeteria has been converted to a senior citizens center, and the gym is an event site for the city, with plans for growth of both.

The Forest Hill Academy continued until 2004, when it closed due to lack of funds. "The problem was we just didn't have enough money," Holloway said.

Holloway doesn't have second thoughts of those years fighting busing to integrate schools. He continued his cry demanding less federal government control as a U.S. congressman from 1987 to 1993 and in statewide public office; he currently serves on the Louisiana Public Service Commission. "You're better off letting people blend on their own than trying to force them," he said.

Louisiana Nursery Festival

To raise funds for the private Forest Hill Academy, in which most of the students were sons and daughters of nursery owners, the idea arose to host a nursery festival in Forest Hill. "A bunch of us sat around in a circle, and we thought out ideas about what we could do to make a large fundraiser for the private school," said nursery owner Marcia Young; "99 and 9/10 percent of us were backing the private school and also in the nurseries, so we said, 'Why don't we do something where we would promote the nursery industry, plus the proceeds could go to the private school.'"

The inaugural festival was held April 11–13, 1986, with Nashville recording artist Peggy Foreman as the featured performer. There were four hundred exhibit booths featuring seventy area nurseries selling plants and garden items, plus art, crafts, food and carnival rides.

From the beginning, the Louisiana Nursery Festival was a family-friendly event with no alcohol sales, said Holloway, who ran the festival in its early years. In addition to the booths and rides on the festival weekend, the event featured an official poster with artwork by local artists and high school students. Past events have included dances, performances by live bands and a parade through town. "It's a good clean festival," he said. "It's a nice festival. It has a dual purpose."

The first year was successful, with profits benefitting the school, so the festival continued. When the academy closed its doors years later, proceeds from the festival were then used to support the Forest Hill Volunteer Fire Department.

Now one of the longest-running festivals in Louisiana, the event attracts thousands each spring, with many of the wholesale nurseries opening their doors to the public in addition to many participating on festival grounds. Booths still number in the hundreds, with all kinds of plants to be purchased, from Cajun hibiscus and other specialty hybrids to ground covers and trees.

The Nursery Festival allows visitors the chance to peek inside the massive industry, said Mike Salter, who owns Living Color Nursery. "They get to see first-hand how plants are grown and where they come from," Salter said in a 2013 article in *Cenla Focus* magazine, adding that nursery owners are willing to share knowledge about the plants with festival attendees.

Highways 112 and 165 become clogged with festival-goers, but Forest Hill residents are relaxed about letting people park in their driveways, along the sides of roads and in nursery parking lots, said Ann Jeter, 2014 festival chairwoman and president of the Central Louisiana Nurserymen's Association. "Forest Hill is really bulging that weekend with people," Jeter said. "Either highway you take there's going to be traffic. We try to accommodate everyone. People here don't get upset about people parking in their driveways."

CHAPTER 10

Forest Hill Today

Forest Hill's population has grown steadily since its inception in 1897, but it still falls below 1,000 people; the population listed in the 2010 census was 818. Still, that number represents an almost 80 percent rise since 2000. The median household income clocks in at $36,667, with the median income for a family at $42,292. About 13 percent of the population live below the poverty line.

The recession of 2008 took a toll on the nursery industry, especially since most nurseries in Forest Hill sell to landscapers and commercial developers. When the real estate market declines, so does the demand for landscaping products. Nursery owner Clyde Holloway believes that about 30 nurseries closed or sold out, reducing the number from 250 nurseries in 2005 to about 220 in 2014. Marcia Young estimates the drop to be closer to 20 nurseries, with most of those being small businesses, but concurs that the number stands at about 220.

There is a definite link between nursery profit and the economy, nursery owners say, with the housing and commercial property markets affecting sales. For Stanley Young, who ships to several southern states, one of his biggest markets is Georgia, which was deeply affected by the 2008 recession, he said. "Georgia has been good except when the housing market fell through. Usually everything we sell ends up in front of a business or a house."

However, when people have less money to spend, they tend to not travel as much and start thinking about their backyard, said Marcia Young. "Gardening in the state has picked up."

Harold and Estelle Poole. *Cheré Coen.*

Mike Salter, owner of Living Color Nursery in Forest Hill, was optimistic about both the nursery industry and the economy in a 2013 *Cenla Focus* magazine article spotlighting the Louisiana Nursery Festival. "The nursery industry has taken a turn for the better," he said, "especially concerning the economy."

TODAY'S NURSERY BUSINESS

Sam Stokes and his wife, Donna, carry on the nursery that his great-grandfather Samuel Stokes began in 1901, and they still sell those popular pansies. Sam's parents, Rodney and Doris Stokes, who ran the nursery for many years and helped it grow to the current size, help out on occasion, along with the Stokeses' daughter, Dana Maria Stokes Lyles, and her husband, Michael Lyles.

A young Sam Stokes stands beneath the grafted tree of his great-grandfather Samuel Stokes. Sam and his wife, Donna, now run the nursery. *Sam Stokes.*

Like their predecessors, they aren't getting rich selling plants, and the job's not a nine-to-five operation, with customers calling and dropping by at all hours any day of the week and plants needing constant attention. "This isn't an occupation," said Sam Stokes. "This is your damn life."

They sell retail in a large area in front of their nursery, just off Highway 112, one of the closest nurseries to Interstate 49. In the spring, there's a rainbow of colors greeting customers—begonias, petunias, impatiens, marigolds, vincas, zincas, coleus, sweet pea vines, bougainvilleas, ferns, lantanas and summer vegetables. In the fall, the tables are lined with cabbage, Brussels sprouts, collards, broccoli, onion sets, shallots, pansies, flowering kale and cabbage, snap dragons, roes and dianthus, among so much more. The Stokes sell seed packets as well.

"It changes every year," Stokes said of their plant offerings, adding that they grow things out of season to have plants ready for customers to put in the ground when the appropriate time comes.

Sam Stokes got into the business in a roundabout way. His father knew a man at Wilco who hired Sam and sent him to El Dorado, Arkansas. It was there that he met Donna, and the two eventually decided to return to Sam's homestead and start working in the nursery business. They started operations in 1977 with help from Sam's parents but no assistance from the government, as Stokes says proudly, including during intense cold snaps, when the federal government provided low-interest loans.

"We like where we are, what we are," Stokes said. "We're a mom and pop type. We're as big as we want to be. We're pretty lucky people."

Following are a few of the nursery owners who call Forest Hill home today.

SCOTT KELLOGG'S NURSERY

Scott Kellogg worked in his parents' nursery during high school and after graduation in an effort to learn the business. After a few years went by, he asked his father, Dean Kellogg, where he would be in ten years if he stayed at Dean's Nursery. "His reply was, 'It depends on what you plant at your house,'" Scott Kellogg said. "He said, 'You can't make a living working for someone else.'"

Like nursery owners before him, the trick was learning the trade on existing nurseries while building an inventory on the side. "So, my second job started," Kellogg explained. "I would work on building my own after I worked for him all day. And it grew. I had to go back and forth. They were only a mile apart. And my parents didn't mind too much. I used their good credit to get the materials I needed. As my business grew, it became too much for me to handle by myself."

Kellogg quit Dean's Nursery and started Scott Kellogg's Nursery in 1995. He sells landscaping plants to NASCAR tracks and famous football stars, singers and actors, he said. Meanwhile, his parents, Dean and Ann Kellogg, have retired. "I think he [Dean Kellogg] enjoys retirement more than I have the nursery business," Scott said with a smile. "This business has its ups and downs."

Jeter's Nursery and Liners

J.J. Jeter's father was a laborer, working in the region's sawmills. His mother wrapped pansies for Sam Poole. The family lived "three miles out in the woods" when Jeter was a young boy, in a house that his father built from leftover scraps of wood from the Duck Saw Mill. The shotgun home offered a wooden stove at its heart, with a reservoir on the side, kerosene lamps for lighting at night and an icebox. Water had to be carried in from a well one mile away until the family had its own. Food included fresh meat from animals hunted from the woods. All four girls and three boys took a bath from one tub, each in turn. "Unfortunately, the last two kids who took a bath had to take the bath and dump out the water," Jeter said.

Jeter milked the cows and fed the hogs before school and then walked almost a mile to class, but he and his siblings "never missed a day," he said. He went to work at Poole Brothers at age thirteen and again after he returned from a sixteen-month tour in Vietnam. While working for Sam Poole and his nursery, Jeter grew liners on the side. His wife, Ann, worked for Poole Brothers in propagation. "Combined, Ann and I have about fifty-eight years at that nursery."

Today, the Jeters own their own business, Jeter's Nursery and Liners, contracting liners for other nurseries. Most of their stock involves shrubs, blueberries, hollies and azaleas. Life has improved since Jeter's childhood and the nursery business is a lucrative one, but the work is both demanding and long, he said. "Together, we work twenty-four-seven."

FOREST HILL NURSERY, ECO NURSERY

Stanley Young no longer owns the vast nursery on Highway 112, having sold the land to Elizabeth Welch and Eco Nursery in 1999. In 2004, Young started brokering plants as Forest Hill Nursery, transporting as many as 200,000 plants per truckload to Louisiana sites and neighboring states. Today, Young moves about $1 million in product, he said, but it's not an easy business. "It's been a laugh," he said. "I've enjoyed it, but it's been hard work."

Welch's Eco Nursery is probably the closest to the heart of Forest Hill, with acres of trees, shrubs and flowers dotting the landscape off Highway 112 next to the town's businesses and city hall. "We are thrilled to have acquired the nursery that Stanley Young established 30 years ago," Welch told *Cenla Focus* magazine in 2013. "We hope to carry on the tradition he started—service with a smile and beautiful plants with lots of variety. Being just one block from downtown Forest Hill makes it easy to shop with us."

YOUNG FAMILY NURSERIES

Mention Doug Young to Forest Hill residents, and they recall an affable man driving through town in a red jeep, with his dog Roscoe in the back seat. "The dog lived sixteen years," said Marcia Young, Doug's wife. "He became a community fixture. Everyone knew Roscoe."

Young was a Forest Hill fixture as well, building an expansive nursery business while working for the Louisiana Department of Social Services until he retired in 1997. With partner and wife Marcia, the nursery grew to be one of the largest in Forest Hill and the South, operating on hundreds of acres under four names: Doug Young Nursery (DYN), Young Hollow Nursery, Liriope Factory and Rio Verde Nursery. The company's main office is located off U.S. Highway 165 near the town center.

Doug Young died in 2009, a loss to the Forest Hill community. "Doug enjoyed his grandchildren, his granddog, his work, entertaining family and friends at home and relaxing to Andrea Bocelli at his lake house on Indian Creek, and traveling, especially to Costa Rica," read his obituary in the December 21, 2009 *Alexandria Town Talk*. "In the last two years, he

Marcia Young. *Cheré Coen.*

had visited Europe numerous times and loved taking in the world's culture (including Italy, Germany, Spain, England)."

His charities included St. Jude's Children's Research Hospital, the Alexandria Zoological Park and the former Forest Hill Academy.

"Doug was always an innovative thinker, who was not afraid to try a new idea if he felt it had merit," the obit read. "He was the first nurseryman in the local area to experiment with contract labor on repetitive jobs which allowed him to monitor cost of production more closely. He was also the first in the local area to utilize a sales staff, and the first to dedicate an entire operation to the 'mass market' production of plants. A lot of Doug's experiments are now common practice in the Forest Hill horticulture industry."

Marcia Young carries on the business with help from her children. Doug Young Nursery (DYN), the only one of the four open to retail customers, is so impressive that it offers visitors a map. Plants are shipped around the country and to agents who sell to big-box stores such as Walmart, Lowe's and Home Depot.

Young Hollow Nursery focuses on monkey grass and border grass, also contracting to companies that sell to big-box stores. The Liriope Factory south of Forest Hill focuses entirely on liriope. "That's all we sell," said Young. "It's bare root, and we sell it over the world. We ship it to Europe, South America, all over the states."

Rio Verde, a few miles outside Glenmora and in Forest Hill, is owned by family members, with employees owning about 40 percent. The two primary buyers are DYN and Young Hollow, in addition to the private buyers. "My husband bought that shortly before he died to let employees have an interest in a nursery," Young said. The company specializes in ground cover, shrubs, perennials and trees to the wholesale market.

In addition to running a nursery, Marcia Young has also run the town. She served fourteen years as mayor of Forest Hill.

RICHARD'S NURSERY

Mike Polakovich has also served the city as a city councilman, fire chief and mayor pro tem for two months. His nursery sells a few items to the public but mostly caters to landscapers from New Orleans, Baton Rouge, Texas, Mississippi and Tennessee, he said. His son, Chris Polakovich, has joined him in the business. His daughter, Cathy Jo Polakovich, had graduated Ohio College and was living north of the Mason-Dixon when Dad called to ask if she, too, wanted to work for the nursery. "She said, 'I'll be there tomorrow,'" Mike said.

From left: Chris, Inez, Mike and Cathy Jo Polakovich. *Cheré Coen.*

Richard's Nursery includes twenty-five hothouses filled with ginger, philads, sacco palms and other tropical plants. There's also a few pineapples growing, a personal project started after a family member brought home a pineapple from Hawaii.

The list goes on and on. Larry Bates specializes in grafting camellias, offering more than 250 cultivars. Bill Thomas of Thomas' Nandina Farm sells about ten varieties of hydrangeas and three varieties of nandinas.

And still there are some looking to learn the business and start their own establishment. Debbie Head worked in the banking business, while her husband sold cars. They bought Poole Brothers Nursery in 1999, expanding the business from 23 acres to 250. "We love what we do," she told *Cenla Focus* magazine in March 2013. "It's not so much a job when you get to do what you love every day."

THE FOREST HILL EXPERIENCE

For many people living in southern Louisiana, Forest Hill remains *the* place to shop for plants. Mention Forest Hill to gardeners and landscapers, and they'll point out flowering shrubs and towering trees across Louisiana as the town's horticultural offsprings. Most people also find working with Forest Hill nurseries to be preferable to dealing with larger commercial operations.

When Sheldon Blue returned home to Lafayette after years working as a contractor in Washington, local landscapers wanted to charge him $12,000 to landscape his yard. "I got a Penske truck, and I rode ahead to get a map of the Forest Hill nurseries and who handled what," he explained. "After visiting four to five places, I got just what I wanted."

The nurseries honored his Washington wholesale contractor's license and rode with him from site to site to help him with his plants. Blue returned home, acquired topsoil in town and planted everything himself. "What they wanted for $12,000 we did for $1,300, plus the sprinkler system," Blue explained. "We had fun doing it, and we respect them for their generosity towards us. Everybody was so nice, and we got it all done in one day."

"I bought many plants at Miss Mary's, twenty-plus years ago," said Donna Christianson of Lafayette. "Miss Mary was an elderly lady who had a small nursery alongside her home along the highway into Forest Hill. She always wore a straw hat and garden gloves. She had amazing roses. I paid one dollar each for my hydrangeas. They are a traffic stopper now, forming a large border under my oak tree and hiding a 'secret' garden. Doug's [Doug Young] and so many other great places—I rode through acres in a golf cart with my girlfriends, laughing and having a blast. Great memories."

Betsy Palmer operates a small nursery, selling plants out of her Lafayette driveway on Saturdays, products propagated from her personal collection. She visits Forest Hill every spring, stopping at BWI and B&T Grower Supply

Richard's Nursery today. *Cheré Coen.*

distributors to pick up nursery supplies and fertilizer, and then enjoys lunch at Mi Tierra in Forest Hill or Fuzzies in Glenmora, she said.

> *My afternoon is always reserved for a leisurely trip to DYN* [Doug Young Nursery], *a 150-acre paradise of outdoor plants and greenhouses hidden in the middle of a large piney wood," she added. "There is no bigger joy for me than driving between dozens of greenhouses, stopping numerous times, dodging puddles and wet, sandy clay to find an entrance, then stepping into the steamy warmth of each structure and racing up and down the rows of plants picking out favorites and making a 'to go' pile on the center sidewalk. I am very like a kid in a candy or toy store. When I'm sure I've seen everything, I load up the car with my pretties and move on to peruse the next greenhouse. We only stop shopping when we cannot fit another plant, whether gallon or four-inch pot, into the vehicle.*

CHAPTER 11
Notable Forest Hill Residents

For its size, Forest Hill has more than its share of notable citizens, from a member of Congress to a National Book Award winner. Here are some of the more famous residents of Forest Hill.

KIMBERLY WILLIS HOLT

Multi-published author Kimberly Willis Holt was born to a military family while stationed in Pensacola, Florida. Throughout her lifetime, like most military kids, she moved around. Her parents, however, hailed from Forest Hill, as had numerous generations before them, so the central Louisiana piney woods was always home. "It felt like home because we always went back to Forest Hill," Holt said.

When she turned fourteen, her father received a short-term assignment in Washington, D.C., one that would end with his reassignment to the New Orleans area. Rather than uproot the family for nine months, the family moved in with their Forest Hill residents while her father headed to Washington.

Holt attended Forest Hill High School and was surrounded by cousins, who showed her around and took her swimming in Tanner and Hurricane Creeks. On Saturday nights, she could hear the stock car races from the

Louisiana Speedway while chasing fireflies through the yard. On Sundays, she attended Elwood Baptist Church, where Clyde Holloway, currently a nursery owner and Louisiana Public Service Commissioner, taught her Bible studies. At Christmas, she went caroling.

Those nine months left a deep impression on Holt's heart. "I feel like it was such a big part of my life," she said. "Forest Hill was the kind of place that when people are sick, they care about you. It was a community that's rich—I think they know how lucky they are. I would ask kids, 'You know you're from someplace special,' and they would nod."

Her parents grew up in the Elwood community, with her father working for the Holloway Nursery. Her grandfather was a postman who would return home with items people left in their mailboxes for him. Her grandmother was an Avon lady. They would love visiting Vivian's Vittles, a town restaurant owned and operated by Vivian and J.B. Butter. "My grandparents would go eat there because the food was so good."

Holt is descended from Reverend Joseph Willis, the first Baptist preacher to settle in Louisiana west of the Mississippi River. Born a slave in North Carolina, Willis established churches in St. Landry Parish and then Rapides Parish, including the Occupy Baptist Church near Pitkin, the Spring Hill Baptist Church near Forest Hill and the Amiable Baptist Church near Glenmora. Holt's grandfather attended the Amiable Church. "That was an interesting person [Reverend Joseph Willis], what he had to overcome and the things he did in settling here," she said.

Holt's first book was *My Louisiana Sky*, a novel for young readers that was later made into a movie. Her second novel, *When Zachary Beaver Came to Town*, won the 1999 National Book Award for Young People's Literature. Almost all of her stories are set in towns based on Forest Hill, and one, *Part of Me*, makes no pretense where it's located. Her upcoming book, *Dear Hank Williams*, is set in a town called Rippling Creek, but again, it's actually Forest Hill.

"Anyone who does research on me knows it's Forest Hill," Holt said. "Setting comes first for me. I really think people are different depending on where they live. It shapes them."

For Holt, she doesn't hesitate to say that Forest Hill shaped her. "Everybody has got their well—artists and writers—that they keep pulling from, and Forest Hill is definitely one I keep pulling from," she said. "I have such sweet memories not just of the times I lived there but the times I went back. Forest Hill's a really special place, and I'm so glad it's a part of me—and always will be."

Clyde Cecil Holloway

Clyde Cecil Holloway was one of seven children growing up at the "very end of Blue Lake Road" in Forest Hill. Their parents taught them strong work values, Holloway said, and were married seventy-one years, one reason why the Holloway siblings still live in the area—five still on Blue Lake Road—and visit each other weekly. "We're just a really close family," Holloway said.

Like most Forest Hill residents his age, Holloway worked in the nursery business for men such as Robert Young and Fred Adams. After attending the National School of Aeronautics in Kansas City, he began working for National and Pan-American Airlines in his early twenties, first living in New York City, where he met his wife of forty-five years. The couple returned to central Louisiana, where Holloway started a nursery in 1968 and, like many Forest Hill nurserymen his age, continued his full-time job working for the airlines, this time at Fort Polk. While at the military base, he would pick up used metal cans from the mess hall to bring home for use as plant containers. Metal cans dipped in tar were popular in the Forest Hill nurseries before plastic containers. "Even when I was at Fort Polk working for the airlines, I picked up the No. 10 cans," he said.

Today, Holloway owns one of the largest nurseries in central Louisiana, shipping twenty-five to thirty trailers of product each year to neighboring states and as far away as New Jersey. His nursery consists of twelve plots of land scattered throughout Forest Hill, in pieces mainly because large swaths of land were hard to come by, he said, due to timber companies owning most of the larger acreage.

Holloway entered Louisiana politics in the 1980s, serving in the U.S. House of Representatives from 1987 to 1993 as the first Republican of the twentieth century to represent north Louisiana in Congress and winning in a district that was traditionally about 85 percent Democratic voters. After the boundaries of Louisiana Congressional districts were adjusted following the census of 1990, Holloway's district was abolished. Holloway has appeared on ballots in Louisiana twelve times.

In October 2006, he received an appointment by President George W. Bush as the U.S. Department of Agriculture's state director of Rural Development, a position he filled until January 20, 2009. On April 13, 2009, Holloway won a seat on the Louisiana Public Service Commission for the Fourth District and was elected to a six-year term with no opposition in 2010.

His primary office on U.S. Highway 165 in Forest Hill—located on what was once "Silk Stocking Avenue"—was built by town pioneer Joseph W. Melder in about 1891.

Irma Rodriguez

Irma Rodriguez marked ten years living in Forest Hill in September 2013. She owns the popular Mexican restaurant Mi Tierra, which has garnered numerous accolades; its walls are covered in magazine features and memorials of her 1997 participation in the Festival of American Folklife at the Smithsonian Institution in Washington, D.C. Three trophies dot the front counter, the most awards won by any contestant in the 2013 Delta Hot Tamale Festival in Greenville, Mississippi. Rodriguez is a pillar of the Forest Hill Hispanic community, and she chalks it all up to God.

Vera Cruz native Irma Rodriguez married a man living as a legal resident in Ferriday, Louisiana, but to reunite with her husband, she had to be smuggled into America. After breaching the border, the group of immigrants got lost and wandered for nine days without food and water through the wilds of southern Texas.

Rodriguez made it to Ferriday but her marriage wasn't a happy one, being marked with abuse. After living with her husband for nine years, her son, Eddie Ponce, called the police, and Irma and her children entered a women's support program.

She moved back to Mexico and married again before ending up in Natchitoches, where she worked for years as a bakery cook and manager in places such as Walmart, Brookshire's and Winn-Dixie. Rodriguez made excellent cakes and pastries, and after doing some research on the Hispanic community of Forest Hill, she suspected that there was a market for her creations. She stopped at the local Mexican food mart and asked if she could sell some of her *tres leches* cakes on a Saturday afternoon, but the owner suggested the local Catholic church instead. For two weeks, Rodriguez baked cakes and froze them; then she gathered them up one weekend and drove into Forest Hill. "I gathered like twenty-two cakes and children's cookies and put them in the back of my truck," she said. "I told Eddie, 'Let's go to Forest Hill. We're going to the church and we're going to sell these.'"

On the way from Natchitoches to Forest Hill, Rodriguez began having doubts. She looked over her shoulder to her handiwork and wondered what she would do with all those cakes and cookies should they fail to sell. She closed her eyes and asked God for a sign.

Rodriguez and Ponce attended Mass and then approached Father Pedro Sierra of Our Lady of Guadalupe Mission about selling the pastries. At first, Sierra was hesitant since the mission sold its own foods for church fundraisers, but Rodriguez offered a cut for the church and he agreed. "It wasn't even ten minutes and I sold every cake there," she said. It was the beginning of a remarkable relationship.

Charmed by her creations, Forest Hill residents began calling and asking for cakes. Rodriguez would drive in every two weeks or so delivering goods, until one day she passed an empty gas station on Highway 112 and got inspired. She approached the owner about opening a restaurant there, but it took some negotiation. Rodriguez was in the middle of her divorce from her second husband; money was tight, and her credit cards were maxed out from her daughter's gallbladder surgery. She had a cash advance amount left on one of her cards, so she took a huge gamble and opened shop. Like the day in church, God provided. "The very first day I was open—I didn't have no advertising—the very first day until today, God has let the blessings fall," Rodriguez said.

She became friends with members of the Hispanic community, many of whom came to Forest Hill as workers and now own their own nurseries, names such as Vargas and Valle. "They have been faithful customers since I've been open. And I've seen their success. They have worked as hard as I have."

Her current restaurant on U.S. Highway 165 offers a much larger space, serving up authentic Mexican dishes that Rodriguez created. On the wall is her certificate from when she participated in the 1997 Smithsonian Festival of American Folklife, serving up her famous tamales, along with numerous framed articles of recent media coverage.

Jay Chevalier

Jay Chevalier wasn't out to endorse or ridicule Louisiana governor Earl K. Long when he wrote "The Ballad of Earl K. Long." After spending four years in the Marine Corps, Chevalier entered Louisiana College in Pineville, majoring in speech and drama, but left to enter the Jimmie Rogers Country Music Festival talent contest in Meridian, Mississippi. He placed second but won the attention of a recording company. But things didn't progress until he wrote and recorded the "The Ballad of Earl K. Long" with the Recco Record Company of Shreveport.

The twenty-three-year-old singer had just finished a song for the Marksville sesquicentennial when a friend convinced him to try pop music, according to the September 3, 1959 article in the *State Times* of Baton Rouge. At the time, hit singles included Johnny Horton's "The Battle of New Orleans" and Stonewall Jackson's "Waterloo." At first, Chevalier ignored the idea. "Then I jumped in my car and started driving," he told the *State Times*. "Three miles down the road, I thought of the chorus. Seven miles—I had the first verse. It was a natural. Later I stopped and played the song for some highway workers. They all liked it."

Governor Long received national attention with his colorful antics both within politics and his personal life, not to mention his time spent in a mental hospital. Chevalier's song "The Ballad of Earl K. Long" became a hit, selling about 100,000 copies. The record's B-side was a song on the founding of Marksville. Not too long after the ballad hit radio airwaves, Chevalier visited Governor Long when he was hospitalized with stomach issues. "You know, he reminds me of a Marine sergeant who would fight to the end to gain his objective," Chevalier was quoted as saying in an August 29, 1960 *State Times* article.

Chevalier also wrote and recorded "Billy Cannon," about the LSU football star who ran eighty-nine yards for a touchdown against Ole Miss in 1959; "Castro Rock" and "Krushchev and the Devil," both songs dealing with the Cold War; and "Rock & Roll Angel." He performed in Las Vegas as Jay Chevalier and the Louisiana Lineshots in the 1960s and 1970s and worked as a consultant on the film *Blaze* with Paul Newman (about the last years of Governor Long and his love interest, Blaze Starr) and on *Cobb* with Tommy Lee Jones. He penned the Southern Legacies Press book *Earl K. Long and Jay Chevalier: When the Music Stopped* in 2003.

More recent songs by the rockabilly performer include "Come Back to Louisiana," named the "Official State Recovery" song by the Louisiana legislature. "Jay Chevalier shall be known as the Official State Troubadour for the Hurricane Katrina and Hurricane Rita Relief Efforts as he travels the world bringing awareness of the destruction caused by the hurricanes and the continuing needs of the people of Louisiana," wrote Louisiana State Representative Danny Martiny.

The Lecompte native who was raised at Midway and attended school in Forest Hill and who grew up "poor and naked in the piney wood hills along the banks of Bayou Boeuf" was named the first Official State Troubadour of Louisiana and was inducted into the Rockabilly Hall of Fame, the Louisiana Music Hall of Fame and the Louisiana Political Hall of Fame.

Robert Wayne Bates

Robert Bates served as a U.S. Secret Service agent under Presidents Lyndon B. Johnson, Richard M. Nixon and Gerald R. Ford Jr.. He also provided security for Vice President Spiro T. Agnew, First Lady Mamie Eisenhower, Secretary of State Henry Kissinger and the Johnson and Nixon children while they attended college. He accompanied President Nixon on his 1972 trip to China, finishing his career in 1976 as agent in charge of the Shreveport field office. In 1986, Bates helped produce a record with fellow Forest Hill native Roger Wright titled *Heroes of Vietnam*.

Today, Robert Bates runs a plant nursery in Forest Hill. He was inducted into the Louisiana Political Museum and Hall of Fame in Winnfield in 2005.

Forest Hill Churches and Cemeteries

Forest Hill is predominantly Protestant, with a long Baptist history. Reverend Joseph Willis was the first Baptist preacher to settle in Louisiana west of the Mississippi River, and he established the Amiable Baptist Church in 1828 near Glenmora, Occupy Baptist in 1833 and the Spring Hill Baptist Church in 1841 on Spring Creek near Forest Hill.

"Spring Hill Baptist Church was established by Cheneyville residents," wrote Wanda Johnson in *Homecoming, a History of Pisgah Baptist Church, 1889–2006*. "Its membership regularly moved for winter months to Beulah Baptist in Cheneyville." The church was torn down after the Civil War, Johnson wrote, but was rebuilt near Forest Hill.

There were several issues affecting Baptists during that period, Johnson noted, including little contact between Baptists east of the Mississippi and west, a division caused by Campbellism and an "anti-mission movement among Baptists themselves, resulting in defection of a few churches from the missionary Baptists."

Fourteen members of the Spring Hill congregation members broke off and started a new church on June 9, 1889, at Smith's School House east of Tanner Creek. Later, they built a church and cemetery on land donated by the Spencer and Crowell Lumber Company. The first pastor, Brother W.A.J. Odom, suggested the name Pisgah—thus Pisgah Baptist was born. The first building was dedicated in 1910 but burned down after World War I. "The site was moved to Paul Cemetery, where there was an available building," Johnson wrote.[100]

Elwood Baptist Church is located in the community of Elwood, just outside Forest Hill. *Cheré Coen.*

Liberty Hill Baptist Church was founded in about 1876 to serve the region's African Americans and is located on Butter Cemetery Road. Forest Hill Baptist Church began in 1900, and Reverend W.B. Marler of Milford organized Elwood Baptist Church on August 24, 1912, with nine members. When Pisgah Baptist Church burned, members held services at the Elwood schoolhouse while a new church was being built. Later, the Pisgah congregation moved to its current home on Louisiana Highway 112.

"The church was the settler's contact with the outside world," wrote Johnson. "Family members were baptized, married and usually buried in the church cemetery. Meetings with others were centered in the only public building in beginning settlements. Singing conventions, suppers, and graveyard workings were occasions for get-togethers."

A group of Belgians settled on Spring Creek near Elmer in 1834 and were visited by horseback by Reverend Robert Duggan, Alexandria's first resident Catholic priest, according to Roger Baudier Sr. in *The Catholic Church in North Louisiana.*

"While Father Figari served Alexandria, 1844 to 1848, a chapel was built on Spring Creek," wrote Baudier. "The carpenter was W. Verheyden, a nearby farmer. All lumber used for the church altar and pews was sawed at a nearby water-powered sawmill and planed by hand. The statues installed were those that the Belgian colonists had brought from Europe, including the life-size statue of Our Lady. All of these and the first altar-stone are now at St. Peter's Church at Elmer, successor of the pioneer chapel of Spring Creek."[101]

The Spring Creek church continued to be served by Alexandria priests, who would travel to the Bayou Boeuf and Woodworth areas on horseback or by wagon and stay at the homes of local residents. In 1878, Sophie Lamoth Martin donated land for the first church, part of the Kanomie Plantation on Bayou Boeuf, also called Martin's Sugar Bend Plantation at Chickamaw. It was completed in 1881 and was located next to the plantation owned by William C.C.C. Martin.[102] In 1899, the church was moved to Lecompte to be closer to its growing congregation. Today, Our Lady of Guadalupe Mission, part of St. Martin Parish and the Alexandria Diocese, serves the Hispanic community of Forest Hill.

FOREST HILL CHURCHES

Calvary Baptist Church
Elwood Baptist Church
Forest Hill Baptist Church
Forest Hill United Pentecostal Church
Liberty Hill Baptist Church
Our Lady of Guadalupe Mission
Pisgah Baptist Church
Pleasant Hill Baptist Church
Tall Timbers Baptist Center
Trinity Christian Center

FOREST HILL CEMETERIES

Brewer-Moore Cemetery

Located off Elwood Road about a half mile from the intersection with Blue Lake Road, an unimproved dirt road leads to this small cemetery containing graves mostly of the Brewer and Moore families, dated between 1850 and 1900. The abandoned Henderson Cemetery, with Henderson graves dating to the early 1900s, is located just beyond. Other names in the Brewer-Moore Cemetery include Rougeau/Rougeot, Rutledge, Davis and Fisher.

Butter Cemetery

One of the largest cemeteries in Forest Hill at more than one thousand interments, Butter Cemetery was created by Henry Butter of England, who moved to the Forest Hill area in the 1840s. His home still exists about a half mile down Butter Cemetery Road. The cemetery rests on land once owned by the Butter family, with an addition donated by the H.E. Duck family.

Cemetery Cockrell Creek

This rural cemetery, once known as Beaver Cemetery, is located in dense woods and is difficult to find; it is about two to three miles off Highway 112, southeast from Midway. Forest Hill pioneer and lumberman Benjamin H. Randolph is buried here, as are members of his family. Other names include Austin, Blankenship, Bonoil, Burns, Cheek, Harper, Holland, Roberts, Rogers, Selby and Simpson.

Graham Cemetery

The Graham family cemetery is located near the original Graham homestead at the end of Bell Road off U.S. Highway 165, neither of which is open to the public. Other family names represented here include Buckaliew, Burlington, Dyer, Moffett and Willis.

Gunter Cemetery

The Gunter Cemetery is listed on Findagrave.com with the following interments: Eddie Dewayne Gunter, Eddie William Gunter Sr., Eddie William Gunter Jr., Hattie Clark Gunter, Wilda Delores Vidrine Gunter and William Michael Gunter. The location is unknown.

Liberty Hill Cemetery

Past Butter Cemetery on Butter Cemetery Road is the Liberty Hill Cemetery, connected with Liberty Hill Baptist Church. This small African American cemetery, with a hurricane fence around the property, contains concrete slabs or vaults and several unmarked graves.

Martin Springs Cemetery

This old cemetery, dating back to the nineteenth century, is located immediately behind the Strange Cemetery on Martin Springs Road, but it is less accessible than that cemetery. William C.C.C. Martin is buried here, along with other Martins and related family members. Martin's Sugar Bend Plantation and the springs that bear his name were located nearby. Names include Compton, Duffel, Hanna, Lamothe, Reeves, Rutherford, Strange and Whitehead.

Paul Cemetery

Forest Hill resident Robert Paul was walking near his home and found a lovely tree to sit beneath. He mentioned to others that he wanted to be buried there, and in 1874, his family laid him to rest in the tree's shade. The Paul Cemetery, located on Perry Road with signs to guide the way, grew around Robert Paul's grave with hundreds of interments.

Pisgah Cemetery

The original Pisgah Church and Cemetery was created on land donated by the Spencer and Crowell Lumber Company. The church has since moved to Highway 112, but the cemetery remains. To reach Pisgah Cemetery, take Blue Lake Road to Pisgah Cemetery Road. The cemetery is located at the road's end and contains numerous interments.

Roberts Cemetery

Roberts Cemetery (also known as Indian Creek Cemetery) is located on Fish Hatchery Road and contains about seventy interments.

Strange Cemetery

The Strange Cemetery is located on Martin Springs Road, with an old iron fence enclosing the area. Immediately behind the cemetery is the Martin family cemetery. Other names for the Strange Cemetery include Carnal and Duplissey.

Willis Flats Cemetery

The Humble Church (also known as Bethel, Humble) was established in 1947 in memory of Reverend Grover C. Willis, the church's first pastor. The cemetery is located on Willis Flat Road.

Notes

Chapter 1

1. Whittington, *Rapides Parish, Louisiana*.
2. McManus, "History of Clifton Community."
3. Works Progress Administration, *Description of Small Towns and Agricultural Communities*.
4. Ibid.
5. Northup, *Twelve Years a Slave*, 74–76. Northup describes his time in central Louisiana as being in Avoyelles Parish, even though it includes an area just north of present-day Forest Hill and Lake Cocodrie.
6. Brister, *Once Upon a River*.
7. Eakin, *Rapides Parish History*.
8. Ibid., 56.
9. Northup, *Twelve Years a Slave*, 68.
10. *New Orleans Item*, "Rock Island to Build Spur at Alexandria," April 22, 1907, 2.
11. Eakin and Lecompte Commission, *Lecompte*, 2.
12. Johnson, *Compton Cemetery*.
13. Ibid.
14. Young, *Historical Sites, Markers, Statues, Etc.*
15. Eakin and Lecompte Commission, *Lecompte*, 3.

16. Head, *Biographical and Historical Memoirs*, 587.

17. *War of the Rebellion Atlas*, Plate CLVI, Baylor University Library.

18. Forest Hill High School Reunion Committee, *FHHS Memories, 1912–1966*, 5.

19. Young, *Historical Sites, Markers, Statues, Etc.*

20. Salling, "Louisiana Jayhawkers."

21. Block, "Some Notes on the Civil War Jayhawkers."

22. Johnson, "Homecoming, June 25, 2006"; various sources.

23. *State Times*, June 2, 1936, 5.

24. Writers' Program of the Work Projects Administration, *Louisiana*.

Chapter 2

25. Finch, Young, Johnson and Hall, *Longleaf, Far as the Eye Can See*, 8.

26. Ibid.

27. Kerr, *Tales of the Louisiana Forest*.

28. Ibid., 1.

29. Eakin and Kimble, *Northup Trail through Central Louisiana*.

30. Smith, *Tale of Three Sawmill Towns*, 2.

31. Forest Hill High School Reunion Committee, *FHHS Memories, 1912–1966*, 5–8; various newspaper accounts; Young, *Short History of Town*.

32. Forest Hill High School Reunion Committee, *FHHS Memories, 1912–1966*, 8.

33. Related by Everett Lueck of the Southern Forest Heritage Museum.

34. *St. Louis Lumberman*, "Progressive Lumber Enterprise in Louisiana," 64.

35. Smith, *Tale of Three Sawmill Towns*, 9.

36. Burns, *History of the Louisiana Forestry Commission*; various sources.

37. *Times-Picayune*, December 8, 1905, 13.

38. *Southern Forest Heritage Museum & Research Center Museum Tour Guide*, 13.

39. Arizona Paths, "History & Culture of McNary."

40. *Town Talk*, "The Town That Pulled Up Stakes and Moved," July 16, 1967.

41. Ibid.; Everett Lueck.

42. Works Progress Administration, *Description of Small Towns and Agricultural Communities*.

43. *Southern Forest Heritage Museum & Research Center Museum Tour Guide*.

CHAPTER 3

44. *Rapides Parish Louisiana Resources and Facilities*, 24.
45. Ibid.
46. *Times-Picayune*, September 25, 1919, 5.
47. Forest Hill High School Reunion Committee, *FHHS Memories, 1912–1966*.
48. *Times-Picayune*, October 26, 1919, 37.
49. Ibid., February 2, 1920.

CHAPTER 4

50. *State Times*, June 22, 1936.
51. Ibid., 112.
52. Sonnier Family Tree, Ancestry.com.
53. Forest Hill High School Reunion Committee, *FHHS Memories, 1912–1966*; Young, *Historical Sites, Markers, Statues, Etc.*; newspaper accounts.

CHAPTER 5

54. *Rapides Parish Louisiana Resources and Facilities*, 13.
55. Ibid., 14.
56. Alexander State Forest Headquarters Building, National Register of Historic Places Database.
57. Barnett and Burns, *Work of the Civilian Conservation Corps*.
58. Alexander State Forest Headquarters Building, National Register of Historic Places Database.
59. Ibid.
60. Ibid.
61. Barnett and Burns, *Work of the Civilian Conservation Corps*, 3.
62. Ibid., 59.
63. Writers' Program of the Work Projects Administration, *Louisiana*, 607–8.

64. Ibid., 4.

65. *Official Annual of District "E" Fourth Corps Area.*

66. Ibid.

67. Works Progress Administration, *Description of Small Towns and Agricultural Communities.*

CHAPTER 6

68. Forest Hill High School Reunion Committee, *FHHS Memories, 1912–1966.*

69. Ibid.

70. *State Times*, September 23, 1940, 11.

71. Atkinson and Tilley, *Camp Claiborne.*

72. *A Camera Trip through Camp Claiborne.*

73. *Rapides Parish Louisiana Resources and Facilities*, 58.

74. *Times-Picayune*, Aug. 3, 1941, 31.

75. 761st Tank Battalion website.

76. Weider History Group website.

77. 761st Tank Battalion website.

78. *Times-Picayune*, January 10, 1946, 2.

79. National World War II Museum website.

80. Ambrose, *D-Day June 6, 1944.*

81. Stanford Computer Science, "Higgins Boat."

CHAPTER 7

82. *Baton Rouge Advocate*, April 28, 1949.

83. *Town Talk*, "Gunter Indicted for Manslaughter by Jury in Forest Hill Shooting," April 29, 1949, 1.

CHAPTER 8

84. *State Times*, "It's Hard to Tell There's a Recession in Bloomtown," December 21, 1980, 45.
85. *Town Talk*, July 29, 1979.
86. Country Pines Nursery website.
87. *Louisiana Life*, "The Nurseries of Forest Hill," 1995–96, 50.
88. Manger, *Mexican Community of Forest Hill, Louisiana*; various sources.
89. Manger, *Mexican Community of Forest Hill*, 4.
90. *CENLA*, "Forest Hill's Million Dollar Baby," 1990.
91. See *History of the Central Louisiana Association of Nurserymen*.

CHAPTER 9

92. Eakin and Barber, *Rapides Parish*; *Town Talk*, July 20, 1980.
93. Eakin and Barber, *Rapides Parish*, 132.
94. *Town Talk*, "Poland High 'Crown Jewel' in Rapids, Says Principal," July 12, 1980, A1.
95. *Town Talk*, "Sign on School Gate at Forest Hill Now Only Visible Reminder of Furor," May 20, 1981, A1.
96. Eakin and Barber, *Rapides Parish*, 134.
97. *Times-Picayune*, "'Squatters' School' Principal Quits," September 28, 1980.
98. *Town Talk*, "Lee Praises Forest Hill for 'Standing Up to Tyranny,'" June 13, 1981.
99. GreatSchools website.

APPENDIX

100. Johnson, "Homecoming June 25, 2006."
101. Baudier, *Catholic Church in North Louisiana*, 16, 21–22.
102. Laurent, *From This Valley*, 263.

Bibliography

Books

Alexandria Daily Town Talk Centennial Edition. Alexandria, LA: McCormick & Company Inc., 1983.

Ambrose, Stephen. *D-Day June 6, 1944: The Climactic Battle of World War II*. New York: Simon & Schuster, 1995.

Atkinson, Cecil, and Kathy Tilley. *Camp Claiborne*. Forest Hill, LA: Ack Hill Publishing Company, 1990.

Barnett, James P., and Anna C. Burns. *The Work of the Civilian Conservation Corps: Pioneering Conservation in Louisiana*. Asheville, N.C.: U.S. Department of Agriculture Forest Service, Southern Research Station, 2012.

Baudier, Roger. *The Catholic Church in Louisiana*. New Orleans: Louisiana Library Association, 1972.

———. *The Catholic Church in North Louisiana*. Compiled in commemoration for the Centennial of the Diocese of Alexandria. Alexandria, LA: Diocese of Alexandria, 1953.

Biographical and Historical Memoirs of Northwest Louisiana. Chicago: Southern Publishing Company, 1890.

Brister, Elaine Holmes. *Once Upon a River: A History of Pineville, Louisiana.* Baton Rouge, LA: Claitor's Publishing Division, 1968.

Burns, Anna C. *A History of the Louisiana Forestry Commission.* N.p., n.d.

Butah, Ivan L., and Reverend W.B. Marler, with W.H. Smith, clerk. *Elwood Baptist Church, Rapides Parish, Louisiana: First Minutes Book, 1912–1922.* Forest Hill, LA: Elwood Baptist Church, 1912.

Butter, Roger. *Camp Claiborne: Only the Memories Remain.* Lafayette, LA: self-published, 2013.

———. *Vittles in the Village.* Lafayette, LA: self-published, n.d.

DeRamus, Troy L. *Up and Down the Red River and Gulf Railroad.* Alexandria, LA: Mpress Printing & Publishing Company, 1989.

DeVille, Winston. *Rapides Post on Red River: Census and Military Documents for Central Louisiana, 1769–1800.* Ville Platte, LA: W.D. De Ville, 1985.

Dill, Harry F. *African American Inhabitants of Rapides Parish, Louisiana, 1 June–4 September 1870.* Bowie, MD: Heritage Books, 1998.

Duncan, Herman Cope, Reverend. *The Diocese of Louisiana, Some of Its History, 1838–1888; Also Some of the History of Its Parishes and Missions, 1805–1888.* New Orleans: A.W. Hyatt Printer, 1888.

Eakin, Sue Lyles. *Crossroads of Louisiana: Where All the Cultures Meet.* Baton Rouge, LA: Moran Publishing, 1981.

———. *Rapides Parish History: A Sourcebook.* Alexandria: Historical Association of Central Louisiana, Kisatchie-Delta Economic Development District Council and the Louisiana American Revolution Bicentennial Commission, 1976.

———. *Solomon Northup's Twelve Years a Slave and Plantation Life in the Antebellum South.* Lafayette: Center for Louisiana Studies, University of Louisiana–Lafayette, 2007.

Eakin, Sue Lyles, and Lecompte Culture, Recreation and Tourism Commission. *Lecompte: Plantation Town in Transition*. Baton Rouge, LA: Venture Productions, Inc., 1982.

Eakin, Sue Lyles, and Marie Culbertson. *Louisiana: The Land and Its People*. Gretna, LA: Pelican Publishing Company, 1982.

Eakin, Sue Lyles, and Patsy K. Barber. *Rapides Parish: An Illustrated History*. Northridge, CA: Windsor Publications, 1987.

Encyclopedia of Forts, Posts, Named Camps and Other Military Installations in Louisiana, 1700–1981. Baton Rouge, LA: Claitor's Publishing Division, 1983.

Field, Martha R. *Louisiana Voyages: The Travel Writings of Catharine Cole*. Jackson: University Press of Mississippi, 2006.

Finch, Bill, Beth Maynor Young, Rhett Johnson and John C. Hall. *Longleaf, Far as the Eye Can See: A New Vision of North America's Richest Forest*. Chapel Hill: University of North Carolina Press, 2012.

Forest Hill High School Reunion Committee. *FHHS Memories, 1912–1966*. Revised ed. Forest Hill, LA: self-published, 1991.

Forest Hill Neighborhood School yearbook 35 (1986).

Head, Wanda V. *Biographical and Historical Memoirs of Rapides Parish, Louisiana*. Shreveport, LA: J&W Enterprises, 1991.

History of the Central Louisiana Association of Nurserymen. N.p., 1986.

Johnson, Richard L., Jr. *Compton Cemetery: An Oasis of Memories Amidst the Great Piney Woods*. Meeker, LA: self-published, 1988.

Johnson, Wanda. "Homecoming, June 25, 2006: Pisgah Baptist Church, 1889–2006." N.p., n.d.

Kerr, Ed. *Tales of the Louisiana Forests*. Baton Rouge, LA: Claitor's Publishing Division, [1980].

Kniffen, Fred B., Hiram F. Gregory and George A Stokes. *The Historic Indian Tribes of Louisiana: From 1542 to the Present.* Baton Rouge: Louisiana State University Press, 1987.

Kramer, G.M.G., and Hope Farrar Kramer. *Rapides Remembers 1875–1975.* Baton Rouge, LA: Franklin Press, 1975.

Laurent, N.B. Carl. *From This Valley: A History of Alexandria, Pineville and Rapides Parish, Louisiana.* Vol. 1, *Prehistory through the Civil War and Village/Plantations to the Present.* Alexandria, LA: self-published, 2000.

———. *From This Valley: An Illustrated History of Alexandria and Rapides Parish, Louisiana.* Alexandria, LA: Red River X-Press, 2008.

Leeper, Clare D'Artois. *Louisiana Place Names: Popular, Unusual, and Forgotten Stories of Towns, Cities, Plantations, Bayous and Even Some Cemeteries.* Baton Rouge: Louisiana State University Press, 2012.

Manger, Dr. William F. *The Mexican Community of Forest Hill, Louisiana.* N.p., n.d.

Marler, Don C. *Historic Hineston.* Woodville, TX: Dogwood Press, 1991.

Martin, Jack B. *Handbook of North American Indians.* Vol. 14, *Southeast.* Washington, D.C.: Smithsonian Institution, 2004.

Northup, Solomon. *Twelve Years a Slave: Narrative of Solomon Northup, a Citizen of New-York, Kidnapped in Washington City in 1841, and Rescued in 1853.* New York: Atria Books, 2013.

Official Annual of District "E" Fourth Corps Area, Civilian Conservation Corps, 1935. Baton Rouge, LA: Direct Advertising Company, 1935.

Partain, Father Chad. *In the Heart of Louisiana: An Illustrated History of Rapides Parish.* N.p.: Historical Publishing Network, 2011.

Rapides Parish Louisiana Resources and Facilities, Survey by the Rapides Parish Planning Board. State of Louisiana, Department of Public Works Planning Division, October 15, 1947.

Raymond, Charles E. *Rapides Parish Pensioners in the War of 1812*. New Orleans: Polyanthos Inc., 1977.

Ruff, Verda Jenkins. *Central Louisiana Families in 1880: A Genealogical Guide to Rapides Parish during the Post-Civil War Period*. Forest Hill, LA: self-published, 1986.

Sibley, John. *Historical Sketches of the Several Indian Tribes in Louisiana, South of the Arkansas River, and Between the Mississippi and River Grand (5 April 1805)*. New York: G.F. Hopkins, 1806.

Smith, T.C. *The Tale of Three Sawmill Towns: Alco, Long Leaf and Meridian, Louisiana*. Natchitoches: Northwest State University of Louisiana Press, 2007.

Southern Forest Heritage Museum & Research Center Museum Tour Guide. Long Leaf, LA: Southern Forest Heritage Museum & Research Center, 2008.

Spearing, Darwin. *Roadside Geology of Louisiana*. Missoula, MT: Mountain Press Publishing Company, 2007.

Spletstoser, Fredrick Marcel. *Talk of the Town: The Rise of Alexandria, Louisiana, and the Daily Town Talk*. Baton Rouge: Louisiana State University Press, 2005.

Stokes, Wilford Perry. *Stokes, a Family History*. Oakdale, LA: W.P. Stokes, 1987.

The Town Talk. *Looking Back: The Early Years in Central Louisiana*. Alexandria, LA: self-published, 2004.

The Town Talk and Louisiana Maneuvers and Military Museum. *The Role of Central Louisiana World Wars I & II*. Alexandria, LA: self-published, 2009.

War of the Rebellion Atlas. N.p., n.d. Available at Baylor University Library.

The What and Where Book of Camp Claiborne, Louisiana. N.p.: Camp Claiborne Public Relations Office Staff, 1943.

Whittington, G.P. *Rapides Parish, Louisiana: A History, a Reprint from the Louisiana Historical Quarterly 1932–1935*. Baton Rouge, LA: Franklin Press, 1970.

Writers' Program of the Work Projects Administration. *Louisiana: A Guide to the State*. New York: Louisiana Library Commission at Baton Rouge and Hastings House, 1941.

GOVERNMENT PAMPHLETS AND REPORTS

A Camera Trip through Camp Claiborne: A Picture Book of the Camp and Its Activities. Brooklyn, NY: Ullman Company, n.d.

Concerning Claiborne. Public Relations Office, Reproduction Branch, Alexander State Forest Training Committee, n.d.

Description of Small Towns and Agricultural Communities Surrounding Alexandria, Louisiana. Baton Rouge, LA: Works Progress Administration of Louisiana, n.d. www.state.lib.la.us.

Eakin, Sue Lyles, and Harvey Kimble. *Northup Trail through Central Louisiana: Beginning at Louisiana State University at Alexandria and Leading through Rapides and Avoyelles Parishes.* Alexandria: Louisiana State University at Alexandria and Louisiana Committee for the Humanities, 1984.

Juneau, Velma. *Belle Cheney Springs.* Lake Charles, LA: Federal Writers Project, Lake Charles District, November 25, 1936.

Louisiana Community Development Block Grant Program Planning Study and Kisatchie-Delta Regional Planning and Development District. *Forest Hill Community Survey and Analysis.* Alexandria, LA: self-published, 1984.

Lueck, Everett. *A Short History of the Red River and Gulf Railroad of Louisiana, 1905–1953.* N.p., n.d.

Roberts, Becky. *A Sociological Survey of Forest Hill.* N.p., n.d. Available at the Rapides Parish Library.

Young, Marcia F. *Historical Sites, Markers, Statues, Etc.* Forest Hill, LA: Village of Forest Hill Mayor's Office, 1996–2006.

————. *Short History of Town*. Forest Hill, LA: Village of Forest Hill Mayor's Office, 1996–2006.

PERIODICALS

Advocate. Baton Rouge, Louisiana.

Blevins, Winnie Mae. "History of Glenmora." *Central Louisiana Genealogical Society* 6, no. 2 (April 1992): 33–34.

Brinkley, Douglas. "The Man Who Won the War for Us." *American Heritage* 51, no. 3 (May 2000).

Colfax Chronicle. Colfax, Louisiana.

David, Herman H. Camp Claiborne newspaper, vol. 1, July 2, 1942–July 3, 1943.

Kossuth County Advance. Algona, Iowa.

Louisiana Democrat. Alexandria, Louisiana.

Lumber Trade Journal. "What the Government Wants in Way of Patriotism and What Manufacturers of Lumber Are Doing for the Government." November 1, 1917.

————. "What the Lumbermen West of the Mississippi Are Doing." March 15, 1917, 27.

Morning Advocate. Baton Rouge, Louisiana.

Pelican Postmaster.

South Rapides Chronicle. Alexandria, Louisiana.

State Times. Baton Rouge, Louisiana.

St. Louis Lumberman. "A Progressive Lumber Enterprise in Louisiana: The W.M. Cady and McNary Lumber Companies—Something of Their Properties and Personnel." July 1, 1913, 64.

Times-Picayune. New Orleans, Louisiana.

Town Talk. Alexandria, Louisiana.

Online Sources

Alexander State Forest and Indian Creek Recreation Area. http://www.ldaf.state.la.us.

Alexander State Forest Headquarters Building. National Register of Historic Places Database, Louisiana Office of Cultural Development, Baton Rouge, Louisiana. http://www.crt.state.la.us.

American Camellia Society. http://www.camellias-acs.com.

Ancestry.com. http://www.ancestry.com.

Ancestry.com, Rapides Parish genealogy board. http://archiver.rootsweb. ancestry.com.

Arizona Paths. "History & Culture of McNary," http://www.azpaths.com/ learn/history/history-culture-lookup.php?City=McNary.

Block, W.T. "Some Notes on the Civil War Jayhawkers of Confederate Louisiana." W.T. Block Jr., Historian. http://www.wtblock.com/ WtblockJr/jayhawke.htm.

Country Pines Nursery. http://www.cpnsy.com.

GenealogyBank.com. http://www.genealogybank.com.

GreatSchools. http://www.greatschools.org.

J., Lizzy. "Bayou Boeuf History" blog. http://bayouboeuflouisiana.blogspot.com.

Kopacki, Ken. Camp Claiborne. http://www.campclaiborne.com.

Louisiana Department of Agriculture and Forestry. http://www.ldaf.state.la.us.

Louisiana Music Hall of Fame. http://louisianamusichalloffame.org.

Louisiana Nursery & Landscape Association. http://www.lnla.org.

Louisiana Political Museum. http://www.lapoliticalmuseum.com.

Louisiana Public Service Commission District Four. http://www.lpsc.louisiana.gov/district4.aspx.

McManus, Jane Parker. "History of Clifton Community—Southwest Rapides Parish." U.S. Gen Web. http://files.usgwarchives.net/la/rapides/cemeteries/clifton.txt.

Melancon, Meredith. "William Ford Plantation and House, Wakefield." Acadiana Historical. http://acadianahistorical.org.

———. "William Ford's Lumber Mill." Acadiana Historical. http://acadianahistorical.org.

National World War II Museum. http://nationalww2museum.org.

Newspapers.com.

Rockabilly Hall of Fame. http://www.rockabillyhall.com.

Salling, Stuart. "Louisiana Jayhawkers." Louisiana in the Civil War. http://www.louisianacivilwar.org.

761st Tank Battalion. http://www.761st.com.

Stanford Computer Science. "The Higgins Boat." http://cs.stanford.edu/
people/eroberts/courses/ww2/projects/fighting-vehicles/higgins-boat.htm.

"Twelve Years a Slave" blog. http://twelveyearsaslave.org/blog.

Weider History Group. http://www.historynet.com.

ORAL HISTORIES

Butter, Roger. January 20, 2014.
Crowell, Richard. January 14, 2014.
Genius, Dale, Director and Curator of the Louisiana History Museum,
    Alexandria. December 7, 2013.
Holloway, Clyde. January 14, 2014.
Jeter, J.J. September 19, 2013.
Johnson, George. September 16, 2013.
Leuck, Everett. February 21, 2014.
Moran, Richard, Curator of the Louisiana Maneuvers and Military
    Museum. October 22, 2014.
Polakovich, Mike. September 17, 2013.
Poole, Harold and Estelle. September 16, 2013.
Rodriguez, Irma. January 30, 2014.
Stokes, Sam and Donna, September 19, 2013.
Young, Marcia. September 17, 2013.
Young, Stanley. September 27, 2013.

ARCHIVES

Alexandria Public Library.
Louisiana Digital Library.
Louisiana History Museum and Alexandria Genealogical Library.
Louisiana State Library.
Louisiana State University–Alexandria Library.

Index

A

Adams, Fred 98, 141
Alco 37, 40
Alexander State Forest 73, 74
Alexandria 11, 13, 19, 22, 23, 24, 27,
  28, 38, 46, 47, 48, 49, 50, 53,
  56, 58, 61, 64, 72, 75, 76, 78,
  80, 83, 84, 85, 87, 89, 96, 105,
  108, 111, 117, 122, 132, 133
American Legion Post 256 92
Amiable Baptist Church 32, 140
Atkinson, Cecil 84, 85, 86, 89, 90

B

Babb's Bridge 27, 28, 29, 30, 38
Bass, Calvin 32
Bates, Larry 114, 135
Bates, Robert Wayne 145
Bayou Boeuf 13, 17, 18, 22, 23, 24,
  26, 28, 33, 35, 36, 64, 67, 145
Beechwood Fish Hatchery 58, 59
Bentley, J.A. 38
Bismark 21, 27, 28, 32, 38, 53
Black Panthers 86
Booker Fowler Fish Hatchery 36, 59
Boom Town 89, 90

Bringhurst 25, 27, 28, 84, 85, 86
Bringhurst, Robert Wilton 24, 25, 85
Brister, Pat 101, 113
Burnum, Winifred 98
Butter, Beulah Virginia 33, 39
Butter, Henry 31
Butter, Roger 27, 28, 31, 53, 55, 57,
  67, 71, 89
Butter, Vivian 71, 140
Butter, William Marshall 26

C

Cady, William M. 40, 48
Camp Beauregard 73, 75, 83, 84
Camp Claiborne 14, 25, 42, 56, 80,
  81, 83, 84, 85, 86, 87, 88, 89,
  90, 92, 93, 99
Camp Evangeline 84
Carter, A.J. 83
Carter, Mary Estelle 94
"Catharine Cole's Letter" (*New Orleans
  Daily Picayune* column) 28
Central Louisiana Nurserymen's
  Association 14, 106, 107, 118,
  119
Chamberlain, Bessie Rovilla 94, 103

Chamberlain Nursery 98
Chamberlain, O.D. "Buck" 98
Chamberlain, Odessa Irene 94
Chauncey Nichols Nursery 114
Chevalier 30
Chevalier, Jay 123, 143, 144
Chevalier, Joseph 26, 30
Choctaws 17, 18, 19, 20, 21
Civilian Conservation Corps 13, 72, 73, 74, 75, 84
Cocodrie Lake 14, 27, 67, 68
Company 4419 Forest Hill 75
Country Pines Nursery 112
Crowell, Caleb T. (C.T.) 40, 42
Crowell, J. Stamps 40
Crowell & Spencer Lumber Company 40, 43

D

Daniel, Willie 47
Dean's Nursery 99, 130, 131
Deaux's sawmill 38
Delaney, Tommy 83
Dentley Plantation 33
DeVille, Winston 21
Dorman, Caroline 49, 61
Doug Young Nursery 32, 118, 119, 120, 132, 134, 137
Duck, Elaine 83
Duck, Ennis Simpson 26, 33, 39

E

Eakin, Sue 17, 23, 24, 25, 121, 124
Eco Nursery 113, 132
E.L. Lacroix Lumber Company 38
Elwood 30, 140
Elwood Baptist Church 26, 27, 30, 32, 67, 140
Evelyn Robbins Nursery 112

F

Field, Martha R. 28
Flitter Creek mill 39
F&M Nursery 116

Ford, William Prince 19, 23, 24, 26, 36, 67
Forest Hill Academy 123, 124, 125, 133
Forest Hill Baptist Church 123
Forest Hill Elementary 94, 121, 122, 124
Forest Hill High School 27, 33, 56, 83, 85, 100, 102, 139
Forest Hill Lumber Company Limited 38, 53
Forest Hill Neighborhood School 123
Forest Hill Nursery 96, 132
Forest Hill School 55
Forest Hill Telephone Company 55, 109
Fort Polk 88, 99, 100, 103, 141

G

Garland Nursery 114
George Johnson Nursery 62, 116
Gifford-Hill Sand and Gravel Company 56
Glenmora 14, 26, 28, 29, 32, 39, 42, 44, 65, 76, 134, 137, 140
Graham, Emily 26
Graham, Julian Dow 32, 83
Graham, Robert 26, 31, 32
Graham, William 31
Gunter, Edward 32, 33
Gunter, Frederick 26
Gunter, Jacob 26, 32, 54
Gunter, Murphy 32, 55
Gunter, Scott 108
Gunter, Wensley Crockett "W.C." 108

H

Halbert, Jody Polakovich 105
Halbert's Nursery 105
Head, Debbie 136
Heroes of Vietnam 145
Hickory Hill Nursery 101, 113
Hillyer, Deutsch and Edwards 39
Hineston 18, 23, 30

Holloway, Clyde Cecil 33, 98, 103, 107, 116, 118, 122, 127, 140, 141
Holloway's Nursery 118
Holt, Kimberly Willis 139, 140
Houston, Central Arkansas and Northern (Iron Mountain) Railroad 38
Hurricane Creek Lumber Company 38, 44, 47

I

Indian Creek Recreation Area 36

J

Jayhawkers 26, 30, 31, 68
Jeter, Ann 102, 106, 125, 126
Jeter, Jonathan Johnetta "J.J." 100, 106, 107, 131
Jeter's Nursery and Liners 100, 131
Johnson, Burrell 26
Johnson, George 62, 80, 93, 94, 95, 98, 99, 100, 102, 103, 106, 115
Johnson, Murphy 105, 114, 116
Johnson, Wanda Ruth 94

K

Kansas City, Watkins and Gulf Railway 13, 27, 29, 37, 38, 53
Keener, Ellen Carpenter 46, 47
Keener, Ganis B. 46, 47
Keith sawmill 38, 44
Kellogg, Dean 99, 130, 131
Kellogg, Scott 99, 101, 130, 131
Kurthwood 42

L

Lamkin, Milford 83
Larry Bates Nursery 114
Lecompte 12, 14, 18, 23, 25, 28, 30, 33, 41, 56, 59, 61, 65, 78, 85, 93, 113, 121, 122, 123, 145

Leper, Clare D'Artois 49
Liriope Factory 132, 134
Living Color Nursery 125, 128
Lockett, Colonel Samuel Henry 22, 23
Long Leaf 13, 30, 37, 38, 39, 40, 41, 42, 50, 51, 55, 90, 91
Louisiana Nursery Festival 14, 124, 125, 128
Louisiana State University-Alexandria 23
Lueck, Everett 13, 41, 42, 91
Lyles, Michael 128

M

Marler, Don C. 18, 37
McNary, Arizona 49
McNary, James Graham 40
McNary, Louisiana 49
McNary Lumber Company 39, 45
Meeker 26
Meeker, Joseph H. 38, 39
Melder 30, 55
Melder, Joseph Wiley 30, 33, 55, 142
Meridian 37, 40, 42
Midway 25, 30, 33, 38, 55, 57, 59, 62, 93, 103, 145
Miller, Willie 47
Mitchell, Billy 14, 64
Mi Tierra Restaurante Mexicano 116, 117, 142
Mizell, Dorothy 57, 83
Mizell, Gordon Dewey 83, 109
Mizell, Thomas Elvin "Nig" 55, 108, 109
Mobley, James 48
Mobley, Lollie Bedgood 48
Morrison, Doris 105
Musgrove, J.J. 47, 48
Musgrove, Mary Ann 33, 59
Musgrove, Reverend Gordon 33

N

Nandina Farm 135
Nash, Leonard 112

Nash, Olivia 112
Nelson, Newton H. 27, 83
Nichols, Chauncey 114
Northup, Solomon 19, 20, 23, 24, 36, 37, 67

O

Occupy Baptist Church 32, 140
Odom, John 26
Odom, Julia 32
Odom, Richard 111, 112
O'Neal, Susan Elina 31
Our Lady of Guadalupe Mission 116, 143

P

Paul Cemetery 57
Peninger, Marion 33
Peninger, Winfard 33
Perry, Reverend Henry O. 83
Pisgah Baptist Church 161
Polakovich, Cathy Jo 134
Polakovich, Chris 134
Polakovich, Keith 105
Polakovich, Mike 100, 105, 113, 134
Polakovich, Richard J. 93, 100, 105, 120
Poole Brothers Nursery 14, 100, 136
Poole, Harold, Jr. 94, 99, 114
Poole, Harold, Sr. 89, 93, 98, 99, 107
Poole, Hayden Johns, Jr. 62, 93, 97, 111
Poole, Hayden Johns, Sr. 14, 64, 80, 93, 103
Poole, Murphy Archie 14, 64, 93, 94
Poole, Samuel Newman, Sr. 38, 93, 94, 97, 100, 103, 131
Poole, Vera Lee 94, 95
Purkey, Margie 80

R

Randolph, Benjamin Hadley 27, 33
Randolph, Juliana 32

Randolph Meeker Lumber Company 39
Randolph, William Fitz 26, 27, 32
Red River and Gulf Railroad 25, 30, 41, 42, 50
Richards, E.E. 38
Richard's Nursery 93, 105, 113, 120, 134, 135
Rio Verde Nursery 132
Roark, W.C. 46
Robbins, Evelyn 112
Robinson, Jackie Roosevelt 87
Rodriguez, Irma 116, 142

S

Sam Stokes Nursery 99, 103
Scott Kellogg's Nursery 101, 130, 131
Shady Nook 14, 65
Sierra, Father Pedro 117, 143
Siess and Ferris Mill 38
Silk Stocking Avenue 33, 142
Smith, Branch E. 38, 40
Smith, Ruth 32
Smith, T.C. 37
Southern Forest Heritage Museum & Research Center 13, 26, 42, 51, 91
Spencer, Alexander B. 40
Spring Creek 19, 24, 25, 26, 28, 29, 30, 32, 38, 65, 69
Spring Creek Academy 24
Spring Hill 24, 25, 26, 27, 32, 38, 53, 55, 140
Spring Hill Baptist Church 24, 26, 32, 140
Spring Hill Lumber Company Limited 38
Spring Hill Ward 25, 26, 27
Squyres, Martha Elvira 33
St. Louis, Iron Mountain and Southern Railroad 41
Stokes, Dana Maria 128
Stokes, Doris Pringle 103

Stokes, Gilbert Rodney 103
Stokes, James Arthur 103
Stokes, Sam 33, 49, 56, 59, 64, 78, 97,
    99, 103, 116, 119, 128, 130
Stokes, Samuel Nathanial, Jr. 103
Stokes, Samuel Nathanial "Nat" 78,
    97
Strange, Milborn Rosalie 78
Stuart Nursery 74
Swearingen, George W. 46

T

Tanner Creek 57, 67
Taylor, Baker 14, 64
Taylor, Harvey 64
Texas Road 23, 24, 25, 67
Thomas, Bill 135
Trinity Christian Center 117
Twelve Years a Slave 24, 36, 67

V

Vallery, Milton 95
Vargas, Francisco "Poncho" 116
Vargas, Migel 116
Vargas Nursery 116

W

Welch, Elizabeth 132
Wells, Colonel Thomas Jefferson 33
Wildcat School 57
Williams, Martha 95
Williams, Nettie 80, 95, 96
Williams Nursery 80, 95, 105, 120
Williams, Shelby 83, 92
Willis, Daniel Hubbard 32
Willis, Dempsey I. 26
Willis, Earl 83
Willis, Reverend Joseph 32, 140
W.M. Cady Lumber Company Limited
    39, 45
Woodworth 14, 18, 38, 50, 58, 73, 74
Writers' Program of the Works
    Progress Administration 20, 74

Y

Young, Charles 32
Young, Douglas 32
Young Hollow Nursery 119, 132, 134
Young, Josephine 32
Young, Marcia 27, 39, 61, 78, 96, 99,
    100, 105, 107, 111, 115, 117,
    119, 125, 127, 132, 134
Young, Robert E. 96
Young, Stanley 96, 98, 99, 108, 127,
    132
Young, Thomas 32
Young, Walter Francis 32
Yowani Choctaws 17

Z

Zimmerman, E.W. 38

About the Author

Cheré Dastugue Coen is an award-winning freelance journalist and author living in Lafayette, Louisiana. A native of New Orleans, Cheré began her career in communications at the 1984 World's Fair and has since written for numerous regional, national and international publications. Her fiction includes historical romances under the pen name of Cherie Claire, as well as nonfiction books *Haunted Lafayette, Louisiana* and *Exploring Cajun Country: A Tour of Historic Acadiana* by The History Press; *Magic's in the Bag: Creating Spellbinding Gris Gris Bags and Sachets* with Jude Bradley; and the cookbook travelogue *Cooking in Cajun Country* with Cajun Karl Breaux.

Josh Coen.

Follow her Forest Hill pages on Facebook and Pinterest.

Visit us at
www.historypress.net
....
This title is also available as an e-book